THE
ART
OF
SELF PROMOTION

BY

Ilise Benun

For permission requests, write to:
Ilise Benun
Marketing Mentor
PO Box 23, Hoboken NJ 07030
(201) 653-0783
www.marketing-mentor.com

Benun, Ilise, 1961 — The Art of Self Promotion.

ISBN-13: 978-0-9791245-0-1   ISBN-10: 0-9791245-0-6

TABLE OF CONTENTS

CHAPTER 1 | MARKETING IS NOT ABOUT YOU

In both personal and professional realms, one of the most challenging tasks is to step outside your own experience and try to understand that of the Other. Likewise, the only way to do effective marketing is not only to know your prospect well, but to see yourself from his or her point of view. This isn't easy, but it's not difficult either.

Listen and Respond

The key is to listen and then respond, and to do that you must step out of the way, put your agenda aside for a moment and actually forget what you want. Give your prospects what they need, not just what you happen to be selling. You might be able to sell him or her something to solve the problem, but then again you might not. Maybe you know someone who can do it better. Remember: it's not about you; it's about your prospect.

Be a Partner

In an issue of @issue: The Journal of Business and Design, George Gendron relates a story about visiting two designers in the same day to discuss the re-design of Inc. The first designer launched into a 2-hour slide presentation of his work, and ended with, "I really hope we get the business." The other designer spent two hours asking about the magazine, its readership, its competition, its future, never uttering a word about design.

Says Gendron, *"The first appointment leaves you with the impression that here's this guy whose got this bag of tricks and he'll apply them in any situation. Whereas, in the second one, you feel like you're signing up a business partner. He wants to understand what you're trying to do...And then, by the way, at the end of the conversation, what would you like to know about my studio."*

Think about the last prospect you met with. Would he or she say you were like the first guy or the second guy?

What your prospects need

You know how sometimes it seems like your prospects want you to have already done their project before they'll assign it to you. Doesn't that seem crazy? Well, if possible, don't take it personally. Your prospect has an image in his mind of what he wants and, very simply put, you need to fit that image. His job may be on the line and he can't afford to take a chance on you if you aren't almost certainly who he needs you to be.

Be a specialist

Nobody trusts the generalist anymore. Your prospect needs you to be a specialist. So, for example, not only do you have to be a graphic designer, but you have to specialize in annual reports or in business cards. Not only do you have to be a travel photographer, but you have to specialize in South East Asia. Not only do you have to be a copywriter, you have to specialize in love letters.

Be professional

Talent is a given, but it's not nearly enough. If you're marketing yourself, we assume you're good at what you do. What your prospects really want to know is: can you work within their boundaries, within their budget, within their time frame? Are you professional or amateurish? Are you stable or fly-by-night? Are you reliable or flaky? Are you flexible or rigid? Are you a hassle-free resource or a Prima Donna?

Be what they need

If you can show your prospect that you're exactly who she needs, that there's a (near) perfect fit, that you can take care of everything, and that the project will go off without a hitch – if you can do all this, in fact, you're in a very powerful position because you have the power to make your prospect look great. And that's what she really wants.

A man I met recently said to me, *"We market, sell, design and build energy conservation projects."* I questioned the order of his verbs. *"Market first, then create?"* I asked. But when he explained to me that he couldn't afford to begin designing or creating his extremely expensive systems until they were sold, I realized that I also do something similar.

Here's how:
I want to write articles about my experience teaching creative writing in the Bronx. I have lots of ideas but I'm not going to waste my time writing an article that my not fit into anyone's editorial calendar. (For that I'll stick to fiction). So I found a few (literally three) magazines that accept articles from teachers and artists. I got their guidelines, studied their rules and sent letters proposing a few ideas that I thought might fit into what I saw. In early August, I got a call from an editor who liked one of my ideas and commissioned me to write an article for their Fall issue, which I did.

Now, it's not always that quick and easy but I had timing on my side. So what about you? Can you target your market first and then create the work with their needs in mind? Without letting it limit you? Can you specialize in more than one thing? I'll bet you can.

Your name is not about you
To begin seeing yourself from your prospect's perspective, think about the name of your business. Whether you realize it, this is your first and foremost marketing tool, and right now it's either working for you or not. If it's not, you could be missing out on opportunities when your name appears somewhere and you're not there to say what it means. Look at it listed in a directory or phone book, or on the attendee list of an industry function. Does it say anything? Does it send a message? Does it send the right message?

What if I called my business *Benun & Associates* or *Benun Consulting?* If you saw this in the phone book, would you know what I do? Probably not. Would you take the time find out? Unlikely, especially if you saw another name you understood better.

Actually, when I began in 1988, I called my company *Creative Marketing & Management;* that's how I described (to myself) what I was doing for people. However, those weren't the words my clients could relate to. I'd watch their eyes glaze over and didn't know what to do. Then, when I started the newsletter, I came up with the words *The Art of Self Promotion,* and suddenly, eyes stopped glazing. Instead, they widened with interest and began to glow. (ok, I'm getting a bit dramatic). I realized that these words mean something to my clients. This is not to say people immediately understand exactly what I do. But they respond with curiosity and, in that first conversation, that's all I'm looking for.

Let your words do the work

Let your name say what you do. Capture the idea in simple terms and let your name actively describe the services provided by you or the product you make.

Let your words be understandable. The print ads for Lucent Technologies show a business card with the tag line: We make the things that make communications work. I like this because it's informal and tells me exactly what they do, without using words I don't understand or telling me more than I need to know. Stay away from big, official-sounding words whenever possible.

Let your words inspire curiosity…especially if what you do is something everyone thinks they understand, like Doctor or Accountant. There's an attorney here in town who says he practices "Hoboken law." Don't your ears perk up at that? Can you translate your run-of-the-mill label into something interesting?

Let your words mirror your prospect's needs. Your words need to resonate within your prospect. Linda Rothschild calls her company Cross It Off Your List, because that's exactly what she helps her clients to do. What exactly do you do? Let your words elucidate, rather than obscure. Avoid abbreviations and acronyms that are incomprehensible. While they may be convenient, they don't speak to your prospect.

Let your words be numerous. Don't hesitate to have a few different names and a few different business cards – one for each hat you wear. They're so easy to create these days, there's no excuse not to. I have four.

CHAPTER 2 | MARKETING IS STRUCTURE

Chances are, if you're running your own business, you don't much like rules or authority, at least not those of other people. You like to do things your own way, use your time as you see fit, create new and innovative solutions for the problems you encounter.

On the other hand, as your own boss, you forgo many luxuries, namely having your work handed to you on a silver platter.

You also do without the structures that a Big Daddy Corporation provides, such as budgets, company policies, and pre-determined prices for your products and services.

In fact, the only structures inherent in working independently are the deadlines you agree to with your clients. So part of your job is to create this foundation for yourself.

We Need Structure

I believe human beings need rules to follow and deadlines to meet. We need agendas to keep us on track and policies to fall back on. We need lists to cross things off of and forms to fill out. We need campaigns to guide us as we approach new markets, plans to help us achieve financial goals. And specific steps to follow, so we don't feel like we're walking into a great big void - even though we are.

Thriving on Chaos?

Now, there are those who claim to thrive on chaos; in fact, you may be one of them. And if structure isn't something you've taken the time to create, then it's a good bet your business isn't running as smoothly as it could. Without generic texts and sample formats, you have to reinvent the wheel every time you want to write a letter, send out a proposal or get someone's contact info.

Without To Do lists and status reports, it's virtually impossible to keep track of where you are on which project, what you promised you'd do or send out or think about.

Without the right organizational tools, I would guess you have projects falling through the cracks, priorities getting shoved to the virtual back burner, and good prospects getting lost in the "system" – or lack thereof.

Structure is the Answer

I think we need structure now more than ever because most of us wear so many hats, play so many roles and offer so many constantly changing services and products.

And I believe the long-term benefits of structure include getting more done, making more money, keeping your clients happy and yourself calm. Doesn't that sound good?

Your Marketing Challenges

Some of the big questions include:

- How to market to corporations
- How to get more (and more lucrative) work
- How to get a consistent flow of new clients
- How to get past gatekeepers to the decision-makers
- How to educate customers about your unique business

Many of the questions have to do with structure, as revealed in this chart.

What you Say	What's in the Way	What you Need	What you Do
I rarely make the time to do my own marketing and can't afford to hire help until we pull in more income. Can't make more money without more help...vicious circle of the small business	Everything	Time	Time comes first. Get to your desk an hour earlier for quiet planning. Choose marketing tools that don't require you to reinvent the wheel every time, like a quarterly postcard campaign that you can plan now, then execute throughout the year.
The period between when I send materials to prospects and when I follow up is just too far apart	Everything	A follow up system	One week to ten days is the ideal interval. By then your material has either been reviewed or been sitting long enough. Schedule one day a week to make your follow up calls and don't let anything get in your way.
I want to create a promo newsletter, I have all the pieces collected and know what to do. I just can't get myself to do it.	Everything	A deadline and the support of others	Make a commitment to someone else about when you're going to get the piece done. Then do it! Pay them If you have to and ask them to check in with you about your progress
I've had seemingly uninterested contacts come through with large projects after 2 years of periodic marketing efforts. Clearly I can't afford to pursue all clients for that long before receiving a response. When do you drop an unfruitful contact?	Everything	To give them a deadline and an incentive	Don't drop anyone completely unless they ask you to. Make an offer with a deadline and give them an incentive. If, after 2 or 3 follow ups, they don't budge, put them on auto-drip to remind them of their interest.

Big Goals and Little Goals

Set a goal for each and every phone call.

You know why you're calling a prospect: to get their business. But as a goal, that's too broad. Before you make a call, take the time to think through what, specifically, you want.

And don't keep it a secret. If your prospect is interested and has time to talk, let them know what you're trying to accomplish. This will allow you to achieve the goal together, a good beginning to any working relationship.

Adapted from The Selling Advantage, here is a fairly generic list of possible goals for each marketing call you make, with space to add your own:

- To find the decision-maker

- To qualify and determine the potential of the prospect

- To find out the prospect's needs

- To introduce yourself and your company, to tell your story

- To get an appointment

- To close the deal

Like a Zoo or a Tight Ship...How Do You Run Your Business?

Have you ever thought about the fact that professionalism is a marketing tool? Well, the way you run your business – the procedures you follow, your fee schedule, your confirmation of terms – all of these structures contribute to the impression of professionalism that will make your clients and prospects want to work with you.

For example, it's essential that your client knows exactly what they're getting for their money. So you should have an agreement stating what's included and what's not, what's extra and for how much, what's due when. All of this clarity is sure to prevent much miscommunication. Because when you don't take the time to spell it out, you pay for it later. And you know it's not cheap!

How to Talk About Money

Addressing the issue of money – a challenge for many self promoters – is a marketing issue because when you broach the subject of money professionally and impersonally (no whining) people feel safe and begin to trust you. And once they trust you, the sale is not far behind.

Often, however, we don't know what to say. So here's the script to get you started talking about money:

- If...you're about to enter into a working relationship but no one has mentioned money yet, say: "Let's talk about money." Or "Here's how my fee structure works..." or "This is how I'd like to proceed," then you outline a few steps, including the financial one.

- If...you don't know what to charge...ask: "Do you have a budget in mind?" Often, they will not, However, whether they know it or not, they probably will have a number in mind which they will not discover until your number doesn't match up.

- If...you don't know how much it's going to be, because this is a new client and you don't know how long the project will take, or how much hand holding they'll need, say, "My fee will be in the range of $xxx" "My fee will not exceed $xx"

- If...you've named your price and there's an awkward silence, say "How does that price fit into your budget?"

Seven Basic Rules of the Office by Jim Magruder

1. **Rise early and start fast.**

    To ensure a productive day, rise early (before the phone starts ringing) and start fast. To build momentum that will carry you through the day, perform simple tasks – send email or draft your daily "to do" list – to get you quickly into the workflow.

2. **Never let fear get in the way.**

    If a client asks you to take on a project that you have never done before, don't let fear of the unknown paralyze you. Stretch yourself; build your portfolio and your capabilities. Look at these challenges as opportunities to grow your business.

3. **Never quote an hourly rate.**

    If you do, clients may silently – and permanently – judge you as too expensive. Instead, offer a flat project fee that will help them budget, and explain that the fee will not vary unless they change the assignment. And be sure to build a little cushion for yourself, especially with a new client.

4. **Quote a price range for every project.**

    Assignments often evolve or change midstream, so quoting a range allows you to charge more without renegotiating.

5. **Always start with a concrete commitment.**

    Never start an assignment, especially with a new client, without a signed contract, purchase order, or deposit. When your client agrees to this, you'll know they mean business.

6. **Bill every project in thirds.**

    This is a sure way to maintain cash flow. Start every assignment with 1/3 down, issue an invoice of 1/3 during the project, and bill the final third at the completion of the project. And be clear that this is your policy.

7. **Thank your clients for every assignment.**
A thank you is just one more way to stay "top of mind." And if you do it by phone, you have a chance to find out their plans for upcoming assignments, and maybe even generate more work.

How to Make Your Marketing Regular

You know how great you feel when you do something regularly: that morning walk or stretching, that daily 15 minutes of creative writing or meditation, that weekly appointment that straightens everything out and forces you to focus on something you otherwise wouldn't make the time for?

Well, it's the same for marketing. So if you want to avoid Feast or Famine, here's what you should be doing regularly:

You should do regular...

- Networking. Commit to 2-3 monthly meetings, educational seminars, workshops and volunteer activities, Instead of waiting for an interesting one to come along, look for events to fill your monthly slots.

- Press release mailings. Send one out monthly or at the very least, quarterly.

- Mailings to "A" prospects. Don't give up on prospects that express interest, but aren't buying yet. Use a built-in structure to keep in touch: a monthly email tip or newsletter, quarterly postcard or calendar.

- Follow-up phone calls: Set aside one day a week to follow up on everyone who has recently shown as interest in your services or products.

And you should have...

- A simple marketing plan...hanging somewhere you can see it and evaluate it monthly (or weekly for the very hungry).

- A marketing budget...Decide what you can afford to spend monthly on marketing, then spend it!

- Forms...Inquiry forms, Order Forms, Mailing List Forms, to gather complete information and to remind you to ask all the questions you need answers to.

- Scripts...for cold calls, follow up calls, voice mail messages and for talking about money with a client.

- Meeting agendas on paper...for your first meeting with a new client or a portfolio presentation.

- Boilerplate text for: Proposals and project outlines, Contracts and Assignment confirmations, Kill Fee schedule or cancellation policy, Confidentiality agreement

Four-Step Formula for a High Impact Thank You Note

You've heard it before – thank you notes are one of the most effective, simplest, and least time-consuming marketing tools you have on your desktop.

But even if the tools are in place, whether beautiful note cards or a standard email message, you still have to figure out what to say, and that's what takes time.

Here's a formula devised by professional speaker, Ron Kaufman:
1. Acknowledge the high level of quality received
2. Report the impact this quality had on the people
3. Explain how the experience exceeded expectations
4. Gesture towards positive interactions in the future

Using this formula, here's a letter he wrote, in just two minutes!

Dear Kunkungan Bay Resort:

I want to thank you for a terrific diving vacation last month. The entire resort is a credit to "environmental tourism" for scuba-diving and for the region.

My friend and I returned to Singapore with nothing but positive comments and stories.

We knew the diving would be great, with unusual creatures on every dive. But we had no idea such great scuba-diving would be coupled with delightful rooms, friendly staff and first class dining that ranks way beyond our expectations.

We will certainly tell our friends about you, and look forward to returning again one day soon.

Sincerely,
Ron Kaufman

Can you see how the simple four-step formula makes this letter so REAL and so effective? Isn't that what you want to do when you send out a letter of compliment or thanks? Now you can do it, in just four easy steps.

CHAPTER 3 | MARKETING IS CONNECTING WITH CLIENTS

When you get a birthday card from a big corporation, does it make you feel special? I didn't think so. You see, they think they have a relationship with you because they know your birthday. But you can't be fooled. That's just technology. And what they have is neither a relationship nor a connection, because big companies can't make a connection. Only people can make connections.

What is a Connection?

When a word becomes a buzzword, we stop listening to it and forget its meaning. That's happened to the word "connection," but it's quite simple. A connection is a link that brings two people together. It's the result of an action you take to initiate or continue a conversation with someone.

Online Relationships

One trend in online marketing is the idea that you can communicate one-on-one with your market, make an "emotional connection" with each person and "build relationships" with people you'll probably never meet.

Through the use and abuse of interactive media, anyone with email and cookies can create what Don Peppers and Martha Rogers, authors of The One-to-One Field Book, call "faux-relationships."

And while I believe it's important to instill trust and create relationships with clients, you can't make an "emotional connection" with everyone who crosses your path.

In an article called. "Relationships, Don't Kid Yourself," Nick Usborne writes that all relationships are not equal. We have close personal ones and distant technological ones; our relationships with our customers fall somewhere in between.

According to Usborne, what is most important is this: your customer dictates the depth of the relationship, which must be based on what he or she needs.

In short, you can't force people into a level of relationship that may appeal to you, but is of not interest to them. That's why you must match the level of relationship with the actual need.

Keep Connecting

So don't try to bond with every visitor to your Web site or prospect who inquires about your services or products.

Just make your follow-up calls, get to know your customers, then keep getting to know them. If you nurture these connections, over time, real relationships will develop.

How to Make a Connection

At the opening session of a HOW Design Conference, attendees were encouraged to meet ten new people over the three days of the conference. This challenge got me wondering: exactly what does that mean? Were we being asked to simply introduce ourselves? Exchange business cards? Have a conversation, a drink, a meal?

The real question seems to be: "How can you allow 10 new people to make a difference in your business? What do you talk about? How, in essence, do you make a connection?

Five Easy Ways to Make a Connection

1. **Find something in common.**

   It could be in the business arena (such as a trade group you belong to or a favorite business author) or on a personal level (like the place you grew up or a part you played). Anything in common will create a connection that says, "We are not that different from one another," which is the first step toward trust.

2. **Uncover their interests and needs.**

   Don't talk too much. To find out what interests the person in front of you, ask a question, then listen to their answer. Look for the moments in a conversation when they become more engaged. That information will help you connect.

3. **Give before you get.**

   Before you ask for anyone's business card, offer them an idea, a resource, a referral, even a taste of what it's like to work with you.

4. **Ask for what you need.**

   Be prepared to share your own needs with those you meet, so that can offer some assistance to you.

5. **Accept graciously.**

   You may be independent, but sometimes it helps to be a little less so. When someone offers you some advice, an idea or a resource, whether you need it or not, whether you asked for it or not, try to accept it. It will mean a lot to them, and will facilitate a connection between the two of you.

Five Levels of Customer Connection

Think about three of your current clients. In terms of their connection to you, where on this scale would each one fall?

1. **Preference:** *"Let's try them this time."*

2. **Favor:** *"All things being equal, they get the order"*

3. **Commitment:** *"They are our supplier"*

4. **Reference:** *"You ought to work with these guys."*

5. **Exclusivity:** *"No one else has a chance to get a project."*

Though you'd probably like all your clients to be at the 5th level, that's not usually possible; indeed it is rare to find this level of connection, given the competitive nature of most marketplaces. What is important, however, is to discover the current level of connection and to develop strategies for increasing to the next, or at least maintaining the one that exists.
(Source: Creating Customer Connections, by Jack Burke)

Try to find one small thing you share in common with every prospect. Building rapport is important, In North America, finding one thing that you have in common with another strengthens the bond of confidence and trust between buyer and seller.

But remember: you're on a business call. Find one non-business rapport item, chat for a few minutes about it, then get on with your problem-solving business.
(Source: Guerilla Selling Communique, www.gmarketing.com/tactics/daily.html)

Listening to Connect

Listen Between the Lines by Terri Lonier:
We entrepreneurs love to talk. We're brimming with new ideas, unique experiences, and great suggestions that we love to share with anyone we come in contact with. Wind us up, push the button and we'll talk for days. But it's just as important to flip that coin: to listen. Otherwise, we cut ourselves off from valuable feedback that can help us grow our

companies. If all the information is flowing out, it stands to reason that nothing is coming back in.

Here are seven key areas where listening will assist in your business growth:

1. **Listen to your customers.**
    When you talk to prospects, listen as much to what they don't say as to what they do. Human beings transmit a lot of important information through body language and what they leave out.

2. **Listen to your competitors.**
    When you're among a group of your competitors, you often will reap greater benefits if you can keep your mouth closed. Listening between the lines can bring you valuable information about another company's plans, strategies and financial status. You'll only get this if you aren't the one doing the talking.

3. **Listen to your colleagues.**
    Feedback and advice from fellow entrepreneurs can be the most valuable guidance you receive. They understand what it's like to be a solo flyer, and can save you hours of time, thousands of dollars, or headache-producing frustration – but only if your ears are open to their advice.

4. **Listen to your staff.**
    If you have staff, stay tuned to their comments, for those comments can translate into a big boost for your company. These individuals understand your business from the inside out, and often have a perspective you lack because you're running the whole show.

5. **Listen to your family and friends.**
    It's true that we often tune out those we care about most, dismissing their suggestions for solutions to our business problems

with the thought, "What do they know about my business?" In fact, they just might know plenty. Don't forget: They know you better than anyone, and can give you a perspective that you often can't get from anyone else.

6. **Listen to yourself.**
    A good deal of the time, we know the answer to our questions, the solutions to our problems, the step we should take next. But that information will reveal itself only if we can quiet the inner yammering and stop running, running, running to get the next task accomplished. Find a way to discover that quiet space within, and listen to it. Often the answers are all inside, if only we take time to actively listen.

7. **Listen to the world.**
    By listening to what's taking place in the worldwide arena, we can align our companies with the trends that are shaping the global marketplace. The world is only one mouse click away. Listen big to think big.

Make a Connection on the Phone

How important is it for a real person to answer your phone? Here are opposing perspectives on a question that businesses big and small have to answer.

A Human Must Answer by Jack Burke, Sound Marketing:
This is one area where technological advances have failed businesses. Gordon Matthews, the inventor of voice mail, said, *"The biggest mistake is using voice mail as a company's receptionist, forcing callers to work their way through a maze of menus instead of having a human direct the initial calls."*

A business should use automated systems only to provide specific service in an efficient manner, such as to check an account balance or activate a credit card. Voice mail systems are horrible ways to treat business leads that have taken the trouble to contact you.

Here are some tips for choosing someone to answer your phone.

What to look for in an exceptional receptionist:

1. Choose someone who is calm, efficient and professional

2. Choose someone who cares about your business and your customers

3. Choose someone with a great memory and who can identify voices easily

4. Choose someone who can make the customer feel immediately welcome and comfortable

Source: *Nothing Wrong with Voice Mail* by David Baker, ReCourses: Gone are the days when sophisticated clients expect human service at every level. Today, when clients visit your office, they don't expect to find a smiling gentleman on a stool that manually moves the elevator between floors. Elevators are now automatic for good reason: it's cheaper, quicker and doesn't require the idle chatter.

Someday we'll look back and marvel that we actually had real people answer phones.

Everyone says clients hate call attendants and voice mail, but what they hate is getting lost in long menus or not being able to reach a human being when they want one. So if you address both of these items when you configure your phone system no casualties should be expected.

Just as most clients prefer to leave you a voice mail message rather than risk a mangled human message, you'll find that sophisticated clients would rather go straight to your private line, provided that they can do so quickly and also have a real person hunt you down if they don't get an answer.

Here are a few tips to use your automated phone system to keep your clients content:

1. Keep your message simple and keep the human option up front: "Thank you for calling COMPANY. Please press zero to speak with our receptionist."

2. Assign a single person to answer those calls, so that when they do press zero, the phone is answered quickly.

3. Get caller ID for each phone line, in case you need to screen your calls.

Make a Connection through the Mail
The Power of the Personal Note

When you open your mailbox to find a letter that has been hand addressed to you, don't you think, "Someone went to the trouble of hand addressing this. It must be someone I know (i.e. there must be a connection)?" Then, don't you spend more time reading or looking at that piece of mail?

Sometimes it's just another piece of junk mail, but sometimes it really is from someone you know, and what a joy!

Well, a simple handwritten address is not enough anymore; to make a connection, you have to really think about who you're writing to and say something special, original, real.

Every time I send out a new issue of this newsletter, I sit down with a pad of my customized post-it notes (my URL and 800 number imprinted in the corner) and, one by one, I write and attach a really short note to a group of people I've been wanting to contact. Sometimes it's a thank you, an FYI an acknowledgement, or something I've been meaning to say.

It takes a lot of time, but this simple effort speaks volumes and will nurture my connection with these colleagues. In fact, there is often an immediate effect. One editor recently responded to my tiny note by picking up the phone and offering me three different ways to work with her.

An effort that says, "I took the time to think about you," makes a stronger impact than any flashy direct mail piece ever could.

Nurture Your Connections
Make 'em Laugh
No, I'm not recommending that you memorize the latest jokes, but humor does bring down our defenses.

Here's something that works for me:
When I make a follow-up call to someone who has asked for information, my prospect usually hasn't had time to look at the materials (despite the fact that it was urgent when they called to request them). No matter. I just say, "Isn't my package somewhere in that pile on the left?" And it usually is, so they usually laugh. More often than not, this little chuckle softens my prospect's defenses and puts them in the mood to talk with me. Then, making a connection is a cinch.

Connect Thru Follow Up
"The hardest thing for people to understand," says Nancy Roebke, "is that very little real business gets done on an initial contact at networking functions. If you go into the function not expecting to get business, but instead to make contacts, you'll have a far great success rate. I attend many functions and never mention to anyone anything about what I do. I spend the whole time listening and writing notes on business cards.

I understand I am not going to close any sales because these people don't know me. But before I leave, I know a lot more bout them."

Roebke recommends drawing the attention away from yourself and onto your prospect:

"People love to talk about themselves. The conversation should center around THEM – what they do and how they do it, how they got their start, what changes they have seen in the industry – anything about THEM. The goal is to find a reason to follow up.

This follow up may be business or personal. It doesn't matter what prompts the follow-up, as long as it personally matters to the prospect.

It proves that you were listening and that you are willing to give before you receive."

Seize Every Chance to Connect

In his book, Creating Customer Connections, Jack Burke writes, "No one is likely to admit that he or she sabotages sales and marketing efforts by treating customers badly. But every time you neglect to make a connection, every time you choose not to seize the opportunity, you are committing a sin of omission – which is harder to trace than a sin of commission, but can be every bit as destructive."

Think about what you could be doing (but aren't) that would benefit your client and solidify your connection with them. Often it's the little things, like these:

1. Drop a quick note at the moment you think of it.

2. Respond right away to a voice or email message.

3. Address and attempt to resolve problems right away.

By Getting Face-to-Face
Bob Jones, Quality Transmission Service

We have a constant awareness of our customers' skepticism toward the auto repair industry, so it's important that we meet them face-to-face.

A customer will call for a price quote, but often their perception of their problem and its repair is incorrect. So, we encourage them to bring their vehicle in for an initial evaluation.

When the customer is present, we can look them in the eye, listen to them, make notes on a clipboard, reiterate what they've said and ask a few questions. Often, while test-driving their vehicle, a casual conversation will ensue which sometimes reveals more than the initial one. They will relate more of the history of the problem and possible ineffective repair attempts. That information helps us do our job better.

By Teaching
Melinda Galt, Linea Interior Design

I recently realized that my best clients have been my students first. I teach evening classes on interior design at the local university to busy professionals (who are also my prospects). Over the six-week course, they get to know me and at the end, they come to my home for a class party. Often, after learning about the topic and about my work, many decide they don't want to do it themselves and they hire me.

By Giving
Christina Andersen, Flora Design

Last January, I felt that one of my mainstay accounts was drifting away. It could have been a case of paranoia, but I thought, "Let me show my customer how grateful I am for her company's business."

So I delivered one of my favorite dried flower arrangements to her. She was surprised and noticeably touched, which really made me feel great. And I was immediately rewarded for my gesture – two people in the office saw it and placed orders for flowers.

By Being the Best Guest

June Evers, Horse Hollow Press

I have become a regular contributor on Petsburgh USA, a cable TV show on Animal Planet because I think ahead and I do everything I can to make the producer's job easy. Here are my Tips for Being the Best Guest:

1. Provide a list of questions and answers

2. Give them detailed segment ideas

3. Help set up and break down

CHAPTER 4 | MARKETING IS GIVING

A mortgage broker recently confessed to me that he deliberately didn't give his card to a couple who was in the market for their first house. In other words, it was precisely in this couple's moment of need, the moment when they were most likely to be receptive to his offer, that this mortgage broker withheld his services. The reason: he didn't want to appear too pushy.

When you market to your clients and prospects, you want something from them – two seconds of their time, an appointment, a project. That's business as usual, and it's the reason their guard is up; yours would be too (indeed it often is). But the reality is that you need prospects to become customers, browsers to become buyers. So you travel that precarious path between pestiness and persistence, trying not to push too hard for what you want, which is simply the opportunity to do your work. And too often you err on the side of too little self promotion, for the same reasons.

Are you a Selfish Self Promoter?

If you aren't actively promoting your business (for whatever reason - and I've heard some doozies), we could say that you're withholding valuable information from your prospects. We might even call you a "Selfish Self-Promoter".

The Selfish Self-Promoter claims not to have the time for self promotion; instead she hopes the phone will ring. As a result, she needs every prospect to become a customer, because there aren't many on the horizon. The Selfish Self-Promoter is always complaining about what he didn't get out of a certain marketing effort and refuses to give anything away – samples, tips, or time that isn't accounted for. And although the Selfish Self Promoter knows that you have to spend money to make money, he just can't get himself to make the investment, and inevitably, his business suffers.

Be Magnanimous

What if, instead of seeing yourself as a salesperson with an agenda, you envision yourself as the bearer of gifts? What if, every time you tell someone what you do, every time you hand someone your business card, every time you make a cold call, you think of it as offering something they want. Something that will help them move closer to their goals? Don't you think the response would be very different?

If the mortgage broker had seen himself as a giver, and marketing as an opportunity to make their American Dream come true, he might have garnered a new client.

Gimmicks, Gadgets, and Other Tacky Marketing Tools that Work

You know those little knickknacks you fill your bag with at a trade show – pens, mugs, visors, calendars, notepads, alarm clocks, key chains, T-shirts, tote bags, and mouse pads? Well, they may be tacky, but if you choose the right one, these gadgets – otherwise known as ad specialties, premiums or promotional products – can be extremely effective marketing tools.

You see, when it comes to knickknacks, it's not the thought that counts. What you give is more important than the giving itself. They work because everyone loves a free gift, but you choose an item that has these two crucial qualities: 1) it relates to your business and 2) your customers find it useful. It doesn't have to be the latest and trendiest item; it doesn't even have to be original. It simply has to be of value to your prospects and to remind them of you.

Premiums to Stay Away From: Five Rules to Follow

If you're a creative type, you don't want to give what everyone else gives. It has to be unusual. But be careful, think before you go too crazy, and use these guidelines:

1. **Don't encourage negative associations.**
    Sayles Graphic Design sent out a yo-yo with their logo on it, but their catchy headline, "Don't trust your next design project to just any yo-yo," anticipated and neutralized any possible backlash.

2. **Don't give cheap food.**
    Cheese and chocolate make great gifts, but they can be expensive, so you may be tempted to cut corners with quality. Don't. Also, consider the environment of the recipient and think through how your gift will be received (In other words, don't send chocolate to the Midwest in July. It might melt).

3. **Don't send something breakable.**
    Needless to say, a box of broken glass doesn't make a positive promotional statement. If you must send glass, package it really well. And if you send something that has a function, like a pocket flashlight, make sure it actually works.

4. **Don't give an ugly calendar.**
    In theory, a calendar is the perfect premium - everyone needs a new one every single year. The problem is that most calendars are really ugly. Unless you give a special one that people will actually want to put up, giving an annual calendar is a waste.

5. **Don't send your gift to prospects before sending it to yourself.**
    That way, you can work out any kinks.

Business Card Bounty

Everyone knows Networking Rule Numero Uno – Don't go out without your business card – although I'm constantly amazed by how many people don't bring their cards to professional events. (It's some kind of self-sabotage, I think). Your card plays a major role in your prospect's first impression of you, and you don't often get more than one chance.

David Salanitro has an interesting take on business cards. He believes they're essential, yet disposable, and he spreads his around like paper samples. *"They're not keepers. They're scraps of paper that you throw at people. Their purpose is to create a first impression, over and over, to be there at the right moment, not to be kept as an heirloom."* Here are a few tips from Salanitro for making the most of your business cards:

- **Hand them to people when you meet them for the first time.** They'll remember your name better if they see it. Develop this as a reflex and don't be shy if they don't automatically reciprocate. Go ahead and ask for their card. It will help you remember their name, an invaluable marketing skill in itself.

- **Give them to people every time you meet, not just the first time.** This will avoid any embarrassment in case they forget your name. It doesn't matter if they don't keep the card; it will have already served its purpose.

- **Include one in everything you send out —** intro letters, invoices, FYIs, article tear sheets, etc.

- **Carry them everywhere you go.** Put a few in your wallet, especially for those unexpected marketing moments when you meet someone standing in line at the bank or post office.

If networking is the most effective marketing activity – and it is – then your business card is your networking ticket (in fact, Salanitro's card looks like a theater ticket). So whether you're walking the dog or taking out the trash, but especially when you are in work mode, always carry your cards with you. You just never know who you're going to meet and what they're going to need.

Time for a New Card?

It's just a tiny piece of paper, but its value is disproportionate to its size. Because space is limited, the weight of each word on your card is exponentially greater than it would be if it were buried in the middle of a brochure or letter. So if you haven't taken a fresh look at your card, this may be a good time to do so. Your focus may have shifted since you started your business, and if you're as busy as most people, your card doesn't reflect this natural evolution.

Maybe your area code has changed or you want to add your email address or most recent cell phone number. Maybe you need to update your tagline, or to add one. When you're ready to do this, consider these points:

- **Make it look professional.**
  There are no rules about what a business card should look like; just make sure it looks as professional as the work you want to do for your clients. For ideas, look closely at the cards of colleagues and competitors.

- **Make it Clear.**
  You're dealing in a small space, so clarity is essential. Include your basic info, and no more. If anything clutters your card or your message, don't use it. Don't get a logo just because you think it will make you look more official. It won't. Your attitude and behavior are responsible for that.

- **Make more than one card.**
  There's no rule that says you have to fit everything on a single card. We all wear a few different hats, so why not have a card

for each hat? Now that we can print out our own cards, there's no excuse not to. I have three, each focusing on the different things I do.

- **Make it interesting.**
  That will encourage people will take a close look at it. It can be undersize, oversize or printed on an unusual paper stock. If your card is not the standard size, a few people may complain, but I'd watch out for those who can't tolerate any unusual business card.

- **Make it change.**
  Let your card evolve and change as your business changes; don't worry about confusing your prospects and clients. They'll adjust.

Contributing to Your Community while Marketing Yourself

These days, there are more and more needs in each of our communities that are not being met, and a social consciousness that needs desperately to be raised. Now more than ever, we all need to contribute. But when you're self-employed – when you are The Corporation – corporate philanthropy takes on a different meaning. There's no Big Daddy matching your contribution, paying you to volunteer, or training you to mentor at-risk youth. It comes directly out of your pocket - and you feel it.

On the other hand, because you're the boss, you are free to choose a project that simultaneously contributes to the growth of your business and the growth of your community. And while it's true that corporate philanthropy can be an effective marketing strategy – potential benefits include customer loyalty, community goodwill and free publicity – all that really matters is that you do something useful. It will affect your business in ways you can't know or anticipate.

Your Criteria for Giving

1. **Your marketing needs.**

   Focus on projects that tie in with your product, service or target market. This reinforces the connection in people's minds. Balance three factors: who will see your name, where the need is greatest and what you personally care about.

2. **People working together.**

   To get the most out of your contribution, you need to be personally involved with other people. Working on a project benefits the cause, while bringing together a group of professionals to work as a team. Through this process, people get to know each other in a new context and across departmental lines, which is how relationships are formed.

3. **Long-term commitment.**

   One-time projects and events have limited benefits. Instead, volunteer to serve on a board for an entire year so your relationships have more time to develop and more work can be done.

Six Not Necessarily Easy but Extremely Valuable things You Can Do in Your Community

1. **Offer your experience.**

   Few people have more to contribute to the communities than entrepreneurs. There is a tremendous need and opportunity to share your knowledge and expertise with nonprofits that are being forced to fill financial gaps with income-generating ventures.

2. **Train employees.**

   Small business owners can make a contribution by hiring and training those with few (or no) marketable skills. As an incentive, tax laws offer business owners a generous welfare-to-work credit.

3. **Work in the schools.**
   You don't have to be a parent to contribute to the education of our children. Anyone can shelve books in the library, fill in for the secretary at lunch hour, decorate bulletin boards or be a technology consultant.

4. **Do pro-bono work.**
   Doing work for a charity is a great way for a new company to generate portfolio samples, while planting the seeds for a professional reputation.

5. **Get the word out.**
   Visibility is very valuable but many can't afford it. Wigginton's Plumbing Service in Sylmar, CA donates space on their five white trucks to the Missing Persons Program of the CA Dept. of Justice. Next to the company's logo and phone number are enlarged photos of missing children (source: PHC Profit Report) Can you share space on your company vehicle or in your display window?

6. **Donate time along with materials.**
   Nonprofits have pressing needs for computers, but they also need help setting up and training their staff on the equipment donated. Otherwise, it's a wasted resource.

CHAPTER 5 | MARKETING IS STORYTELLING

Have you ever noticed that most news articles draw you in with a tale about one person, while simultaneously illustrating a broader issue? When you hear a speaker at a conference, isn't it when they tell a story to demonstrate their point that your ears perk up? And don't we spend an awful lot of time watching TV and movies, listening to songs, and (hopefully) reading books? Well, these are all based on stories, other people's stories.

We Listen to Stories

We like stories because we want to be moved, transported, maybe even changed, and stories have the power to do this. Good stories fire the listener's imagination. They embolden, enliven, and motivate, not only their creators but all who hear them. They take us out of our own lives and show us other possibilities; when we hear about someone who accomplished a great feat, we think, "if she can do it, so can I." And so we try.

Knowing your company's story actually involves much more than reeling off the corporate highlights (like when the company was founded...) and it can be much more powerful than any marketing pitch. In a perilous economy, a story can serve as a competitive tool that defines a company's place in the bigger picture.

From *Inc. Magazine*:
You don't need any special literary skills to use storytelling as a marketing tool; it is completely natural. Just answer the question, "What do you do?"

with real-life anecdotes and examples of how you've solved your clients'
problems. Bring your story to life by infusing it with your own personality
and a few facts and figures. A little drama doesn't hurt either.

What Your Story Must Have

"The classic business story is much like the classic human story," says
Mark Helprin, noted novelist. "There is a rise and fall; the overcoming
of great odds; the upholding of principles despite the cost; questions of
rivalry and success; and even the possibility of descent into madness."
(In other words, drama). The stories worth telling contain the basic
elements that both engage the listener and remind the company of
where it needs to go.

Be sure to include as many of these elements as you can in your story:

1. **A Simple Truth.**
    Simplify and clarify to articulate what your business really does.
    Boil your mission down to a single, accessible idea. (Here's
    mine: "I help people who hate to promote themselves.") The
    Inc. article refers to it as an Elevator Speech: you must be able
    tot tell the man standing next to you in an elevator what you do
    before he gets off at his floor.

2. **A Strong Passionate Voice.**
    Good stories draw people in, and that requires a storyteller who
    conveys the passion for the business. So add Company Evangelist
    to your job title, and even if you're the shy type, remember this:
    your story is not about you, it's about The Company.

3. **A Mirror.**
    Storytellers engage listeners by providing characters they can
    identify with. Likewise, you want your prospects to see them-
    selves in the characters (i.e. clients) in the stories you tell.
    You'll know when they do because they'll be nodding their

head, knowing that you understand their needs, and that you can help them. If that doesn't happen, it may not be a good match, which is fine.

4. **Drama and Romance.**
   Romance is not just boy meets girl. Romance is adventure. Romance is life – someone else's. The concept for the famous J. Peterman catalog was based on what Peterman called factual romance. Wrote Peterman: "The items, copy and artwork (of the catalog) come together to evoke a sense of glamour and richness of a time that seems more romantic and carefree than today."

Ralph Morrison, Peddler of Encouragement

Ralph Morrison tells stories for a living, and people listen. I asked him how small business owners can use stories in their marketing... Morrison: *"We need to realize that we're telling stories every day. If you have a bad experience at Sears, you're going to tell the story. It's what we do naturally. It's the easiest way to communicate. If we could realize we're already doing it, we could improve upon it."*

To market with stories, you have to turn facts into pictures, because that's ultimately what we buy. People buy convertibles because they picture themselves driving down the road, hair blowing in the wind. A car salesman paints a picture for his prospect. He's selling an image, an experience. He'll say, *"Imagine yourself in this car. Think of how good you'll feel when you pull up to the baseball field and your team piles out."* Your prospect must find him or her self in your story; that's when their imagination comes alive. Once they're engaged, you've got them. That's when they see things as they could be, not as they are. It adds hope, life, and adventure.

What Great Brands Do

A brand is a metaphorical story that's evolving all the time. This connects with something very deep – a fundamental human appreciation of mythology. We all want to think that we're a piece of something bigger than ourselves. Companies that manifest that sensibility in their employees and consumers invoke something very powerful.

Levi's has a story that goes all the way back to the gold Rush. Ralph Lauren is trying to create history. His products all invoke a frame of mind and a persona. You go into his stores and there are props and stage settings – a saddle and a rope. He's not selling saddles. He's using the saddle to tell a story. Stories create connections for people. Stories create the emotional context people need to locate themselves in a larger experience.

Source: Fast Company Aug/Sept 97

How to Tell Your Story

Your story in the media:

Publicity is by far one of the most effective marketing tools at your disposal, but how do you promote yourself to the media so that they will give your growing business the spotlight it needs?

Storytelling.

That's right, because ultimately, business stories are human interest stories and every reporter is looking for a good story. In fact, the press refers to the articles they write as stories. Here are four things you need to give the press to help tell your story:

1. **Personality.**

   "A company is faceless without the people who run it," says Joanne Cleaver, a business writer. "In any story, you want the personality of the people to come through. You want to get a sense of who they are."

2. **Facts and figures.**

   Reporters love facts and figures; they anchor a story in reality. However, if you prefer not to divulge sales figures, talk instead about your rate of growth. Say, "Our sales have doubled in the last year," or "We've already met our sales objective for this year and it's only July."

3. **Anecdotes.**

As impressive as numbers can be, they are not the whole story. Real-life examples of how you solved a client's problems bring your story to life. According to Cleaver, "Readers want to hear about real people, they respond to that. Your story says I've been there." Tell the stories behind the facts and embellish them with details that would make someone want to listen. (This is where drama comes in handy.)

4. **Details that Reveal.**

Reporters have their antennae up for interesting details about the people behind the companies. More and more, that's the approach that reporters are taking. So you need to be open and to share details. Maybe the contents of your refrigerator reveal something insightful about your marketing strategy, or the fact that you work best in your pajamas. "No business experience is a straight line. Your motivation and vision for the business is affected by who you are. Think about the attitudes that have played into your success or your experience," says Cleaver.

Your Story in Advertising

What's the untold story behind your decision to get into the business you're in today? Was it a lifelong ambition? Were you busting your buns for someone else and decided to go out on your own? Was it the inspiration of a family member or friend in the same industry? Or was it just an opportunity that fell into your lap?

Everyone has a story – a potentially interesting story – to tell about how they got into the business they're in. A story that can actually be used to promote the business. Even if you think your particular tale seems mundane, trust me, it can be turned into a provocative hook for an ad that gets people interested.

I once wrote a column about a former social worker who made a rather radical career leap to running a maid service. I suggested she use the headline "Why I gave up social work to rid the world of dust balls" in her ads, followed by her story. It added a lot of curiosity value and established credibility through the real-life element of the message.

Instead of racking your brain trying to think of a grabby ad concept, hook prospects with an interesting first-person story. It will certainly separate you from your competitors. And you'll have accomplished the hardest part of advertising: getting attention.

Source: Jerry Fisher, Entrepreneur Magazine, Feb 1997

CHAPTER 6 | WHAT EXACTLY IS WORD-OF-MOUTH?

A 12-year-old I know found a fingernail clipping in her Chinese food recently and promptly told all her friends to avoid all Chinese restaurants.

I remember seeing the IMAX movie, Everest, and I was so moved that I hounded everyone I knew to go too, and to read "Into Thin Air."

You know the feeling. You're gushing, ready to burst, eager to share, because someone fixed your computer, designed you a gorgeous brochure, repaired your car, or solved a problem you've been living with too long.

Consumers Rely on It.

A full 80% of us make our decisions based on personal recommendations because we desperately need help separating the wheat from the chaff when it comes to music, movies, books, classes, mortgage brokers, financial advisors, babysitters, health professionals, and vets – in essence, any service, product or event that is personal and involves trust.

What is Word-of Mouth?

Word-of-mouth is simple: people talking to other people because they have something to share. It's the trust, faith and knowledge of the person doing the communicating that carries so much weight. And if both sides are not engaged – if someone's talking but the other isn't listening – then it's not word-of-mouth.

How Did you Get It?

Many people think of word-of-mouth as something you get, not some-thing you do, and that if you're getting it, you don't have to do anything. Word-of-mouth is a mysterious combination of high visibility and good timing – and it happens when you are consistently and clearly marketing yourself, when you are "out there." Besides being a marketing strategy, word-of-mouth is the end result of excellent work and persistent marketing. To stimulate word-of-mouth you have to think about who should be talking about you, and what you want them to say. There are proven techniques for airing, encouraging and training these word-spreaders and you'll learn about them here.

Word-of-Mouth is Up to You

Belinda Plutz, of Career Mentors, said, "If you want word-of-mouth, just do good work." Of course, Belinda is right, but good work isn't enough anymore. I don't think you can expect even your most enthusiastic supporters to recommend you without being prompted. It's your responsibility to take action; you must, at the very least, ask them to spread the word, and at the most, make it worth their while to do so.

What Makes People Talk?

Godfrey Harris, author of "How to Generate Word-of-Mouth Advertising," "Don't Take Our Word for It" and "Talk is Cheap," has given word-of-mouth a lot of thought. To see the hundreds of strategies and "recipes" he offers, you've got to get the books. Whatever your business, you're sure to find some great ideas. The following is but a snippet from his perspective.

Seven Ways to Get People to Spread the Word:
 1. Give Something Away:
     Those who receive gifts tend to display them and to talk about those who provide them.

2. **Do Things Differently:**
   Any unusual activity that benefits a customer evokes favorable comments about its sponsors.

3. **Empower Your Customers:**
   Provide those who buy from you with awards and privileges to share with others – a great way to make new friends for your business.

4. **Provide Information:**
   Give your customers new, important or humorous information to share with others. You'll benefit from the discussions arising from the inevitable, "Where'd you hear that?"

5. **Pay Attention to Reactions:**
   How people deal with each and every aspect of your business yields important clues about what they will say about your business to others.

6. **Minimize Negative Comments:**
   No business can fully avoid negative comments – whether deserved or not – but all of us can minimize any potential damage through attentive responses to the problems exposed.

7. **Get it Right:**
   Not only can word-of-mouth be stimulated, it can be sharpened and directed to produce the results desired.

The Difference between Word-of-Mouth and Referrals

I've always used these two terms interchangeably, but Harris makes an interesting distinction. He says, "Referrals are passive, given by people only when asked for help - 'Where did you get that?' Or 'Do you have a good plumber?' - and generally without reward to the person making the referral.

In contrast, word-of-mouth is the result of a proactive program where customers are specifically rewarded for talking."

Three Simple Steps to Stimulate Word-of Mouth
by Michael E. Cafferky

We all do our share of sharing information, but some people are heeded more than others. So who are those talkers and how can you enlist them as your partners in self promotion?

Certain kinds of people - call them your Champion Supporters - are more likely to talk (and be heard) than others. They are self-confident, socially involved, love to tell stories and are sought out for advice. Champions are especially persuasive because they have little to gain by bragging about you.

1. **Find your Champion Supporters.**
    Make a list of people who fall into these categories
    - Experts: They work in your field and provide credible testimony to the value of your products or services.
    - Market Mavens: They like to be current on where to get the best deals or the best value for the money.
    - Influentials. They are connected to the political dynamic of their community (home, work, city, and county).
    - Opinion Leaders: They know others rely on them for advice, so they're constantly soaking up information to share.

2. **Inspire Champions to Brag**
    - Treat them like Champions. Give excellent service, which includes: reliability, safety, durability, responsiveness, access, courtesy, credibility, competence, and communication
    - Educate Champions. They need detailed information about you to share with others. Make sure they understand all there is to know and have materials to pass along.

- Involve Champions. Give samples of your products or services and ask their opinion. Ask them to get the reaction of their friends and report back to you.
- Invite Champions. Set up opportunities for Champions to brag. Organize formal or informal meetings with prospects and get the conversation going.

3. **Thank Them When They Talk**
   - You can never thank a Champion too often for bragging about you. Thank them in person; thank them on the telephone; thank them in writing. Recognition, tastefully and genuinely given, will often result in more referrals.

To Get Word-of-Mouth, You Have to Ask For It

In this article, adapted from a *Working Woman* article by Mary Connors, the author uses "referrals" differently than Godfrey Harris does, but whatever you call them, you won't get them unless you ask for them.

"Not asking for referrals at all is the biggest mistake salespeople and small-business owners make," say consultant, Bill Cates. "They think it's unprofessional; they're afraid to come across as too aggressive; they don't want to jeopardize the existing relationship. But people who ask more, get more."

How then, do you go about getting referrals? You can pay people for leads and you can hit up everyone you know – both strategies are better than not asking at all, though not much. Here are two of the most effective ways:

- **The new client approach.**
  Your stellar qualities are fresh in the mind of a client who's just made the decision to buy from you. So there's no better time to tell this person how much you'd appreciate the chance to serve others just like her.

- **The boomerang approach.**
  Give referrals out and they'll come back to you. A Chicago real estate broker created a Referral Directory of reliable service providers for homeowners and sent it to her A-list. Not only were recipients and those listed grateful, but directory-related referrals resulted in four sales and several listings for her in the months that followed.

Three Ways to Get Testimonials

1. **Ask a specific question.**
   Anne Holland wrote: The best way to get a good testimonial is to ask how your product helps your client get the number one sales benefit you tout. For example, I ask them to fill in the blank after the words: Here's how PR News helps me do my job better and saves me money.

2. **Ask for it in writing.**
   Melanie Deardorff wrote: Testimonials are a powerful tool to use in getting more business...and they're usually yours for the asking. Next time one of your clients praises your company, say. "Can I have that in writing?" Then, use the testimonials in newsletters or brochures, on your web site or on the back of a business card. Better yet, send one out each month with the invoices you mail. The possibilities are endless!

3. **Write it for them.**
   Bob Jones wrote: Sometimes a customer says they will write one, but they don't always follow through. After all, it's a busy world. A seminar speaker once recommended that if you want a testimonial letter, write it for the customer and all they have to do is sign it. By doing that, you will have the letter say what you would like it to, and you will stand a better chance of actually getting it.

Three Ways to Use Testimonials

There is a distinct difference between having others sing your praises and shouting them out yourself. That's why publicity is so powerful. Once you've gathered a few testimonials and chosen the most concise and powerful ones, here are a few fresh ways to use them:

1. **Include testimonials in your proposals:**
   People want information that justifies their buying decisions. Selecting your company is probably a risk for them. So anything you can do to inspire trust and to increase their comfort level will tip the scales in your favor.

2. **Use recorded testimonials "on hold":**
   Instead of piping music into the ears of callers on hold, why not do some subtle selling to this captive audience?

3. **Create a Testimonial Wall:**
   If your product or service requires people to wait around somewhere, you've got a captive audience. Do a soft-sell with testimonials framed on a wall to reinforce their buying decision.

Quantum Quote

"When a new venture does succeed, more often than not it is in a market other than the one originally intended to serve, with products or services not quite those with which it had set out, bought in large part by customers it did not even think of when started, and used for purposes besides the ones for which the products were first designed."

Peter Drucker on Innovation and Entrepreneurship.

CHAPTER 7 | YOUR LIST IS YOUR MARKET (OR WHO ARE YOU MARKETING TO?)

You can make lots of mistakes in direct mail. You can create a terrible mailing package that no one will open. You can set your price too high – or too low. You can offer your products at the wrong time. But nothing is as bad as mailing to the wrong list.

So says Jeffrey Dobkin, author of "Uncommon Marketing Techniques." And in "Power Packed Direct Mail," direct marketing pro, Bob Bly, makes this bold statement: *"A mailing list is more than a means of reaching your market. The list is the market."*

It follows, then, that if your list is your market, you better have the right list.

Commit to a Market

Contrary to what you may want to believe, the whole world is not your market. Even if everybody CAN use your product or service, you can't market to everyone; it's physically impossible, and trying to do so will only waste (and exhaust) your marketing efforts.

Don't let the fact that everybody could be a prospect get in the way of making the decisions to target a specific and identifiable market. In reality, there are only a few specific groups with a need or desire for the special benefits you offer. Your job is to find those "niche" markets and commit your efforts to getting business from them, one at a time. It will not limit you; indeed, it will free you.

Free Lists Online?

Wouldn't it be great if the lists we usually have to pay for were available – free – on the Internet? Isn't free information what the Internet is supposed to be about?

Well, there are some lists floating around out there, and while most of them are unfiltered and by no means comprehensive, they're often a good place to start.

For example, many online versions of the Yellow Pages, give you the same thing you'd get from, well, the Yellow Pages. You still have to call for contact names then enter these names into your database to generate labels.

Even better, as a benefit to members, many trade groups put their membership directories online. You can find your market's association and choose which members you want to contact, and sometimes even link to their web sites.

As for the big mailing list companies, most have web sites, but they aren't giving much away. For a few, you can download mailing lists and databases, which saves time but encourages us to hurry through a selection process which requires clear thought and guidance.

Permission Marketing – Getting Prospects to Raise Their Hands

Marketing is a contest for people's attention and the biggest problem with mass-market advertising is that it fights for that attention by interrupting, which may have been effective years ago, but today there's too much going on for us to permit – much less enjoy – being interrupted. Our natural response is to ignore these interruptions.

According to Seth Godin, interruption marketing has given way to permission marketing, which means that the marketer's challenge is to persuade consumers to volunteer their attention – to "raise their hands" as Godin likes to say – to agree to learn more about a company.

"Permission marketing is based on selfishness," says Godin. "Consumers will grant you permission to communicate only if they know what's in it for them. If they've agreed to pay attention, they don't want you to waste their time. They want you to solve their problems, but first they have to trust you. So you tell them a little something about your products and services, they tell you a little something about themselves, you tell a little more, they tell a little more, and over time, you create a mutually beneficial, learning relationship."

"You still have to get people's attention in the first place, of course, and that still costs lots of money. But that's the beginning of the story, not the end. After you do the expensive job of getting people to pay attention, you have to turn attention into permission, permission into learning and learning into trust. That's how you get consumers to change their behavior."

The point of permission marketing is not just to entertain people. People want to have fun, but I think they also want to learn things that will make their lives better and easier. If your prospects are learning, they'll give you permission to teach them more.

Although the idea of permission marketing is more about mind-set than medium, Godin believes the Internet is the ultimate tool. *"If people get a piece of direct mail and don't respond, you assume that they've rejected your offer. So one of the problems with interruption-based marketing is that you have to assume that "no" means "no" – when, in fact, it usually means 'maybe'."*

"If you send 100 people a letter and only two of them become customers, the cost of asking the other 98 why they didn't is exactly the same as the cost of contacting them in the first place."

"If you want to change behavior, you have to talk to people over and over again. What's so magical about the Net is that the cost of talking to the 'no's' more than once is zero. With email, frequency is free. You can keep communicating with people, keep teaching them, and keep trying to turn them into customers – frequently, quickly, and unobtrusively – so long as they've given you permission to do that."

How to Make your Dream List a Reality

How much would you be willing to pay for a list of people who need what you have – and know it – and who are so close to being ready to buy that they've already made the effort to contact you? Wouldn't that be worth a lot of money? Or maybe even invaluable?

You might call this your Dream List. Or you could call it your In-House List. That is, if you really took the time to develop the best list for your business.

The best list for you is the list of people with whom you have already begun the process of building a relationship. Don't underestimate its value for a minute. These people already know you, and may even trust you (at least more than those on the mailing list you're thinking of renting), which means that the amount of time it will take to make the sale is shorter.

There are two parallel strategies for building your In-House list: in the first, you choose your prospects by compiling names from invoices, business cards and bits of paper and records, attendee lists from networking meetings, etc. The names you want to capture are those of everyone who's ever expressed interest in your work.

At the same time, choose marketing tools that motivate these qualified leads to raise their hands and ask you to market to them – tools like publicity and press coverage, offers of free samples, and email newsletters.

Together, these two strategies produce your Dream List – people who either already know you or whom you've selected to get to know you.

Sounds like a lot of work? It's actually not the complex task you may imagine it to be – it just takes some work and some time. In fact, compiling your Dream List is an ongoing process that can be surprisingly economical and made to fit manageably in your day-to-day routine. Just keep your eyes open and be organized.

Four Simple Ways to get Prospects to Identify Themselves

My most effective list – my Dream List – is the one that keeps growing because every day, people call me or find my web site. Maybe they've seen or read about my email newsletter or it was forwarded by a colleague. Maybe they've even purchased one of my books.

I have no doubt that these people are my prospects; I know they're interested because they've qualified themselves. They've raised their hand and said, "I need what you have. Please tell me more." They've granted me permission to market to them.

Besides traditional publicity, (i.e. getting your name and phone number in the press) here are a few ways you can get your prospects to raise their hand:

1. **Mail or fax-back Reply cards:**
    Send out a simple, one-page letter to 100 prospects chosen from a trade group's directory of members, and include a form that your prospect can mail or fax back for more information. Those who do are warm leads. Be sure to follow up with a phone call to all who take the time to respond.

2. **Offer something free:**
    Run an ad or coupon in a local or industry paper that will motivate prospects to call.

3. **Simple mailing list form or guest book:**
    Keep a simple form handy for prospective customers to fill out when they come in, or for you to fill out when they call you.

Should you Rent a Mailing List?

Renting a list is easy, but choosing the lists that will make your marketing profitable is a different story. Any list broker can rent you any of the thousands of commercially available lists, so make sure your list broker is experienced and able to do a thorough analysis of your target market and objectives before presenting you with list recommendations.

Seven tips for Profitable List Use and Selection -

adapted from "Power Packed Direct Mail" by Bob Bly

1. **Work with a list broker.**
    You can find list brokers and managers online, in the yellow pages or through referral.

2. **Define your target market.**
    It is your responsibility to come up with an accurate, detailed definition of your target market. If you can clearly describe your "ideal customer," a list broker or manager can probably find the right list for you. Be sure that this definition is correct and complete, and as specific as possible.

3. **Don't overlook your own resources.**
    You may have access to directories, attendee lists, subscriber lists, and other sources that list managers don't know about. Compiling and collecting your own list can make sense, especially if your market is small.

4. **Beware of special list offers.**
    Most lists range in cost from $50 to $250 per thousand names. Some response lists may be slightly higher, but beware of anyone who offers you "special" lists for much more than that.

5. **The best lists for business-to-business direct mail.**
   These include trade journal subscribers, trade show attendees and members of professional associations. Also, look for lists of prospects who have demonstrated, through some action, an interest in your field.

6. **The best lists for consumer mail order.**
   Those that include people who have recently bought a product similar to yours at a similar price.

7. **Never rent the whole list at once.**
   Always start with a small portion and test. Then, if successful, you can rent more names and mail more pieces.

Five Tough (but really important) Questions You Should Ask Your List Broker - Before Renting a Mailing List.

Remember that even though you're the buyer, list brokers work for the list owner. So make sure you get tough with them about answering your questions. Here are a few to get you started:

- Precisely who is the list made up of? Does it include actual purchasers or merely inquirers?

- How old are the names on the list? How often is it updated? How recently was it cleaned?

- How recently have the people on the list made a purchase? Ask about "hot names", people who have purchased in the last few months.

- How often has the list been rented? Too often and it may suffer from list fatigue; never and it's not a good market.

- How many mailers have tested the list? How many continued mailing after their test? How many rolled out (mailed to the whole list)?

Source: Uncommon Marketing Techniques by Jeffrey Dobkin

List Rental 101

List Lingo:

If you're going to do this, you should understand as much as possible, and knowing the jargon is an important step in finding quality lists. With the help of AZ Marketing - a list management and brokerage firm in Cos Cob, CT - Target Marketing published this glossary of terms:

Actives: Buyers on a file that have made a purchase over a specified period of time

Continuation: Mailing a larger portion of a list once a smaller portion of the list has been tested.

CPM: Cost per Thousand: charge per 1,000 names rented

Data Card: A printed card providing basic information about a list: size, pricing, characteristics, selects, usage.

Decoy: A unique name inserted into a mailing list to verify correct list usage.

Expire: A customer who has ceased making purchases yet remains on the list.

Merge/purge: Process by which duplicate records are eliminated from within a list or between two or more lists; also identifies multi-buyers among lists being used.

Multi-buyer: One who has bought more than once from the same company or purchased from several companies.

Nixie: An undeliverable name and address.

RFM: Recency/frequency/monetary value: list data which allows the user to select the date and frequency of purchase as well as the dollars spent.

Run Charge: The price charged by a list owner for names run or passed but not used.

Sample Mailing Piece: Example of the material needed to be sent to a rented list; required by most list managers to verify legitimacy and non-competitive offers.

Selects: Criteria used to segment a list: gender, age, recency , etc. Extra charges usually apply.

Source: The origin of the names: space ads, direct mail, television, telemarketing, etc.

Suppression: Pulling undesirable records off a list, such as prison addresses, credit risks, or merely records that don't fit the profile of customers you'd like to reach.

Test: Sample portion of a rented list used to determine the responsiveness of the entire list, usually no larger than 5,000 to 10,000 names.

Universe: Total number of names available on a list within a particular section.

Usage: The history of what other companies have mailed to a particular list.

CHAPTER 8 | TIPS ARE THE FUTURE

Here's what the cover of one national small business magazine promised readers would find inside: Top 150 Low-Cost Franchises, 10 sure-fire businesses you can start today, 8 tips to tackle though customers, 7 smart ways to grow your home-based business and the 3 best ways to start a business. All this on one very busy cover!

We all know what's going on. Time is getting shorter, everything is speeding up and, from my chair, there is no end in sight.

What We Want

We want what we want, when we want it. We want to be successful and to look good. We want to save money. And we don't want to work too hard.

That's why tips are so alluring – they're fast, they're easy, they're digestible, and they promise a quick fix. We like tips because they're action-oriented, and even if we don't actually take any action, they make us feel active. Tips say, "All you have to do is read this short little article and all your problems will be solved." Of course, that's neither true nor possible, but that doesn't stop anyone from hoping.

What We Need

Here's what I need: answers to questions, practical solutions, fabulous resources and short-cuts. I need new perspectives and fresh ideas. And most of all I need rules, directions, and guidelines to follow. That's why I like tips. They are useful and can provide some of this. Tips are often surprisingly simple (and sometimes painfully obvious) ideas that I can implement immediately and without much time, effort or money expended. Tips are Ideas you can "Take to the Bank", according to Target Marketing, a magazine whose articles are almost exclusively in tip format.

Most of all we need time – time to sit quietly and sift through the avalanche of information that bombards us from every angle at all hours of the day. Time to think about the big things and the little things. Time to step back and look at our lives.

Provide tips to your prospects and you'll also be providing a little extra time in their lives.

Show What you Know

The goal of marketing is to make your prospect comfortable enough to say yes to working with you. But while one prospect may need to see a fancy brochure, another may not be comfortable unless he meets with you. Here is what you must understand: underneath it all, your prospects just want to trust you. Use tips to gain your prospect's trust. So don't be stingy. Show them you know what you're talking about. Go ahead and give them a freebie. And don't worry that once they have this information in hand, they won't need you. It doesn't work that way. Information is abundant…it's help that we need.

How to Use Tip Sheets

1. **Tip Sheet Press Release:**
    Editors are on the lookout for information that will be useful to their readers. And like everyone else, they're looking to save time. Turn your press release into a tip sheet and they'll reprint directly from it, often with a blurb about you. Follow this format and chances are you'll get some publicity. And you'll look like the expert.

2. **Tip Sheet Promotional Newsletter:**
Promotional newsletters — both online and printed — are perfect vehicles for tips. However, many newsletters I see give nothing but news about a company, its products and services. Not that there's anything wrong with that, but fluff is less interesting to your prospects than practical ideas and solutions to their problems. A balance of the two can satisfy everyone's needs. So turn your newsletter into a tip sheet and your clients won't be able to throw it away.

3. **Tip Sheet Brochure:**
Besides using my newsletter as a press release, I also use it as my brochure. It clearly conveys my perspective, as well as a sampling of the marketing recommendations I make. By reading it, my prospects can usually tell if they want to work with me. The only thing missing that a brochure might have are the details of how I work, such as fees and specific services offered, which can easily be taken care of either on the phone or in a personal letter.

Top Ten Tip Titles

1. # Ways to save money

2. # Steps to a successful ____

3. How to pick the best ___

4. # Reasons to ___

5. # mistakes to avoid when ___

6. Checklist for ___ success

7. # Sure-fire ways to ____

8. Everything you need to ___

9. Immutable rules for ____

10. Trends you can't afford to miss

How to do How-To's

Tips require action-oriented thinking (quite a challenge in our passive society). Tips are how-to and hands-on. They speak in the imperative; they tell us what to do. They provide nuts 'n bolts, practical information, and whenever possible, solutions. And although they have an air of simplicity, tips are not necessarily simple to write. So here are some tip-writing tips:

1. **Q&A:**

   Don't tell them what you think they should know; tell them what they want to know. Listen to your clients' questions, and then give them answers.

2. **How-to:**

   Do your prospects need to write a resume? Organize a closet? Choose a care-giver? Be a leader? Get on the Internet? Protect their assets? Tell them how. Give them directions, steps to follow.

3. **Myth and Reality:**

   If there are beliefs people hold about your business or industry, show, clearly and concisely, one by one, how these beliefs are not true.

4. **Checklists and Quizzes:**

   Everyone loves a checklist that makes a little extra space in their brain. What do your prospects need to keep in mind?

5. **Troubleshooting:**

   Help your clients help themselves. This is especially useful for product sellers or those who provide a repair service. You might even already have a tip sheet buried in a user's manual. Recycle it into a marketing piece.

6. **Call them:**

   If you still can't think of what your clients and prospects need to know, ask them. I mean it, call them up and ask them.

The Vocabulary of Tips: Mix and Match

Verbs:
- Avoid
- Overcome
- Use
- Get
- Save
- Maximize
- Capitalize
- Guarantee
- Prevent
- Reduce
- Increase
- Remove
- Become
- Clarify

Adjectives:
- Easy
- Cheap
- Free
- Sure-fire
- Infallible
- Authentic
- Immutable
- Money-saving
- Low-cost
- Smart
- Best
- Simple
- Quick
- No-lose
- Win-win

Nouns:
- Steps
- Ideas
- Ways
- Keys
- Tips
- Hints
- Tricks
- Techniques
- Reasons
- Rules
- Secrets
- Essentials
- Strategies

How to Create Eye-Catching, Skimmable Tips

Write an intro paragraph, give your tips, and then summarize with a short closing paragraph.

Use bullets, interesting symbols or numbers to highlight each tip. Give each tip a bolded, 2-3 word (1 sentence max) opening then elaborate on it. Be consistent within the list. If each bolded top starts with a noun, make sure they all do.

Of Course You're an Expert —
Eight Ways to Position Yourself as One in the Media

When your primary business value is your expertise, there is no promoting method more fruitful than utilizing publicity to establish yourself as the "guru" in your field. Expert publicity can be a very potent stimulant for your career.

Become a partner to the media. They need your expertise. In fact, publications and news organizations are in business precisely to provide solid information. As long as your expertise helps them do their job, they will need you as much as you need them. If they don't get the quotes from you, they'll be getting them from your competition.

And for those media reporters who don't use your material at first, it's just as valuable to get on their radar for the next time. If you provide them with solid information when they call, the process can become self-propelling, and you will be called and quoted in many places for a long period of time.

Here are eight steps to promote yourself as an expert:

1. **Pick a topic for a how-to article, one aspect of your expertise-** the more relevant to current problems and/or trends, the better.

2. **Define your target audience and focus your comments directly at them.** Think about what they need to know.

3. **Compile a target list of media that your market watches, reads and listens to.** Get names from reference directories and tune in yourself to make sure there's a match.

4. **Include between five and ten how-to sentences that help your target audience solve their problems.** For example, if you're an accountant, the topic might be "Nine Ways to Save on Taxes for Individuals and Families."

5. **Write in the negative.** This adds shock value, which is more readily picked up by the media. Negatives sell and that's the bottom line for publishers. So the accountant's tips become "Nine expensive mistakes people make on their tax returns."

6. **Make the piece educational rather than sales-oriented.** Editors want to help readers, not print advertisements.

7. **Watch for breaking new stories affecting your industry.** Offer your expertise to the media at those crucial moments.

8. **Don't be afraid to give away a few secrets.** Many people will not do for themselves whatever you're offering to do for them. And it's not because they don't know what to do. So go ahead and tell them what to do.

CHAPTER 9 | LEARNING TO SAY NO

Why do we hate to say no?

Early in my career, I worked for a company whose policy was to never say no. When asked to do something they'd never done before (and didn't know how to do), they'd say yes and then figure it out once they'd landed the job. (They are no longer in business, by the way.) What I remember the most is a frantic energy around the office, an excitement that was contagious, but also extremely draining. There as no room for error, no time to think, no learning curve. And no one doing their best work.

I think we don't say no for reasons that have nothing to do with reality.

The Fear: "If I say No…"	The Reality:
• They'll never call again.	• Maybe, but it depends mostly on how you say no.
• They'll get angry.	• Maybe, but they'll get over it.
• They'll find someone else they prefer.	• Always possible, but generally unrelated to your actions.
• They'll spread rumors and ruin my reputation.	• Unlikely, they have other things to do.

Ten Reasons to Turn Down a Project

Turning down work is easier when business is booming and you've got more than you can handle. But when things are slow, it's tempting to go after jobs, customers, and markets you'd be better off without. Here are some guidelines (adapted from PHC Profit Report) that may help you say no when the pressure is on.

Beware of:

1. **The unknown.**
   If you're in over your head and the job requires you to do something you've never done before.

2. **Large Investments...**
   of time or money with iffy prospects for a timely return.

3. **Stranger Danger.**
   If you know nothing about the customer and the project sounds too good to be true.

4. **Manpower crunch.**
   If the job requires you to make hasty hiring decisions.

5. **Unrealistic Schedules.**
   The job is yours for the asking, but they want it done faster than you've ever done it before.

6. **Dangling Carrots.**
   Don't be fooled by the promise of lucrative future work "if you'll just do this one job for nothing."

7. **Fuzzy benefits.**
   If the biggest benefit is that it'll look good on your client list, it's probably not worth the price you'll pay to do it.

8. **Major mismatch.**
   Your specialty is quality work but your customer is a penny pincher who treats you like a commodity.

9. **Deferred gratification.**
   Saying yes to a project that's not quite right may require you to say no to a better project later.

10. **Bad vibes.**
    Follow your instincts, no matter what words they're using.

How to Decline with Grace

When I was a toddler, saying no was not only easy, it was loads of fun. As I've gotten older, it's become more difficult and considerably less fun. But it's essential to the success of a business. You must say no to some things in order to say yes to others. And sometimes you have to walk away because, while everything else seems fine, the price is just not right.

When you know it would be better for you to say no, here are some possible responses to "Can't you do it for less?":

- Yes, but if I don't maintain a healthy profit margin, I won't be in business the next time you look for me.

- Yes, but I wouldn't be proud to have my name on the work.

- Yes, but you won't be satisfied, and that's all you'll remember.

- Yes, but I wouldn't be able to devote the time and attention your project deserves.

- No, but let's see what we can do within your budget.

- No, but we can make a few changes that might lower the price.

- No, because my prices are based on actual costs. But I can refer you to someone who may be able to do it for less.

Customer Complaints –
Six Ways to Turn Them into Strategic Learning Tools

According to Technical Assistance Research Programs, 26 out of 27 people who have had a bad experience with a company do not complain. And 91% who are unhappy, but fail to complain, do not come back. Why? People assume that complaining will be a hassle, that nothing will be done about it and that it's just easier to go elsewhere.

So how do you find out what needs improvement? Simple: ask. It takes courage to ask for feedback because you don't know what you're going to get. But if you handle a complaint well, you can actually build more loyalty than existed before. You will earn greater respect from your customers and you will learn valuable lessons that will help you to improve your business. You'll hear about what your customers appreciate but never thought to mention, because you never asked. And you may even get a few compliments.

1. **Be open to complaints.** Listen graciously and ask yourself, "What can I learn from this complaint?" Practice not taking it personally.

2. **Develop a system for inviting feedback, in person, whenever possible.** Most people won't offer their feedback unless invited to do so. It's a risk because they don't know how you'll take it. You can cay, "I'm always looking for ways to improve my product/service. Do you have any suggestions?" Or, "If you could change anything about the product/service I provide, what would it be?"

3. **Solve the problem as quickly as possible,** or make good on it by offering to forgive a charge or provide additional services. You want your customers to know they've been heard. Make any policy changes necessary to prevent a recurrence and be on the lookout for related problems.

4. **Listen even more closely to what they're not saying,** or may be afraid to say. This is a different kind of listening.

5. **Don't forget to thank your customers for bringing an issue to your attention.** You might even consider offering a reward or incentive.

6. **Use what you learn.** The easy part is gathering the information; the hard part is putting it to good use. Do what you say you'll do. Don't promise something and then not deliver it, or you'll compound the problem further. Set up a regular time to review complaints and make changes.

Prospects are People –
Ten Things to Understand about Your Prospects

1. **Your prospects need you.**

    Do you imagine that by promoting yourself, you are intruding on or interrupting your prospect? Are you thinking, "They won't want what I have to offer," or "They're probably already working with someone?" Well, as Stock Photography Guru, Rohn Engh, likes to say, "At this very moment, your prospects are waiting for you." If you approach each prospect with that frame of mind, you'll make a better presentation.

2. **Your prospects want to look good.**

    Things are kind of scary out there. No matter the industry, from construction to graphic design, things aren't the way they used to be – not for you and not for them. So what they want from you, over and above what they're asking for, is that you make them look good; that's your real job.

3. **Your prospects are, well, lazy.**

    That means you have to do some of their work: help them find you, help them contact you, and then, of course, help them work with you. The fewer obstacles they have to surpass, the morel likely they are to follow through, and the more likely you are to get the work.

4. **Your prospects have a lot going on.**
Don't lose sight of their big picture. In the office, there are interruptions galore. They can't get anything accomplished, their desk is a disaster area, their voice mailbox is jammed, and their email is stacking up. In a word, things are out of control. You are just one of the many things they are trying to focus on. Now just try to ask: Why aren't they calling you back?

5. **Your prospects act on impulse.**
We all do this: we see something interesting, we get excited, we call for information, and when it comes, we put it in a pile. Determine as quickly as possible if you're dealing with an impulse inquiry and waste as little time as possible with them. Don't write them off entirely; just put them on your quarterly mailing list and let them come back to you. Real needs and desires will stand the test of time.

6. **Your prospects need to pigeonhole you.**
Although you hate it, let them do it; in fact, help them. Give them a box to put you in, and a label to put on your box. (I'm speaking figuratively here). There's plenty of time to tell them later about your full range of services.

7. **Your prospects may not know what they need.**
Listen to them and provide a solution to their self-defined needs. Offer a few alternatives for them to choose from. If necessary, explain, without trying to persuade, why what they say they want might not be the best thing for them. Then let them decide.

8. **Your prospects need time.**

    It's not always a put off. Believe them when they say they have to "think about it," or that they have to sell the idea to someone else. We all need time to think, time to get ready, to adjust, to clear our plate. Give them the time they ask for, and then keep in touch, reminding them that they were interested. And remember that some things will never come to fruition. That's life.

9. **Your prospects are people.**

    Your relationships are not with companies; like it or not, they're with human beings. And relationships are more important now than ever because, with everyone moving around, you better believe they're taking the "Rolodex" along.

10. **Your prospects are just like you and me.**

    Don't forget: you are a prospect to someone out there too. Which defenses do you use? How do you want to be treated when someone's marketing to you? How often do you want someone calling? How much freedom and time would you like to have to think, to ask questions and to make your decision? How do you want to feel about the process when it is over?

CHAPTER 10 | DIRECT MAIL IN THE INFORMATION AGE

Is Print Dead?

Reading all the hype about online and interactive media, you might be inclined to believe that print as a medium is dead – or at least dying. But while there's no doubt that online delivery of information is becoming more and more important, paper communication is far from on its way out.

Consider this:

Print provides universal access to information. To receive your mail, your prospects don't need anything but a moment to focus on it. It's the time that's hardest to come by these days.

Plus, people crave things personal. Direct mail can be intimate advertising or it can be junk. How your direct mail is perceived depends on how well you target your market.

We complain about clutter and we dream about the paperless office. But I think we need pieces of paper, to jog our memory and to remind us of what we think we need.

Mass Marketing is Out

Micro-marketing is in. And not only is it trendy, it's also much more cost-effective. The theory is this: it's better to send something unique and fabulous to 10 (or 20, or even 100) carefully selected prospects, than to send a generic mailing to 1000 unqualified potential customers. Micro-marketing requires a lot more effort on your part, especially in terms of research, but it's worth it.

Direct Mail Doesn't Work

Neither does public relations, advertising, or networking. By themselves, none of these tools work. But, if you put them together and let them feed each other, complement each other, work off each other, then you've got a marketing explosion. Isn't that what you want?

Okay, Write an Intro Letter

I'll say it again: a letter is still the easiest and least expensive marketing tool you've got, if only you could sit down and write the darn thing, right? Well, Bob Bly, a direct mail copywriter, prolific author of marketing books, and subscriber to my newsletter, has agreed to let me excerpt from his intro letters to show you what kinds of copy get a 10% response. Try this as a worksheet.

- **Intro paragraph**

  Often, an intro paragraph can simply be a question that your clients often ask you, or a problem they've voiced. You can even quote your clients. Here's an intro Bob uses: *"It's hard to find a copywriter who can handle industrial and high-tech accounts,"* a prospect told me on the phone today, *"especially for brochures and direct mail."* Do you have that problem?

- **Call to Action**

  In response to the first paragraph, your prospect needs to be nodding her head unconsciously and thinking, "Yeah, me too." That's when you tell them what to do. If you want them to call for more information, say so. If you want them to fax something back or return a postcard, say that. Here's how Bob continues: *"If so, please complete and mail the enclosed reply card, and I'll send you a free information kit describing a service that can help."*

- **The Goodies**

  Tell them what they'll get if they do what you ask. Here's what Bob's prospects get: *"You'll receive a comprehensive WELCOME letter that tells all about my service…my client list…client testimonials…samples of work I've done in your field…a few schedule… even an order form you can use to put me to work for you."*

- **The Solution to Their Problem**

  You, of course, are the solution to the problem identified in the intro paragraph. Describe, very, very briefly and as specifically as possible, what you do and who you do it for. Avoid generalities and things anybody (i.e. your competition) could say. Here's what Bob says to software companies: *"As a freelance copywriter specializing in business-to-business marketing, I've written hundreds of successful ads, sales letter, direct mail packages, brochures, date sheets, annual reports, feature articles…for software companies all over the country."*

- **Case Histories**

  People love to know they're not alone. If you have room, tell a couple short (one-paragraph) stories about how you've helped other clients with similar needs. Again, be as specific as possible.

- **Next Step**

  Put yourself in their shoes and imagine the possible situations they may find themselves in. Here's Bob's version: *"Whether you have an immediate project, a future need, or are just curious, I urge you to send for this information kit. It's free…there's no obligation. and you'll like having a proven copywriting resource on file – someone you can call on whenever you need him."*

- **The P.S.**

  Repeat something, offer something. Either recap what they'll get, present the call to action or say something personal. And include your phone number so it's handy. Bob's PS: *"Need an immediate quote on a copywriting project? Call me at 201-555-1212. There is no charge for a cost estimate and obligation to buy."*

Focus on Personal Letters

The easiest, most inexpensive direct marketing tool at your disposal is still the personal letter – not to be confused with the pseudo-personal letter.

Here's why I still like letters: They're not fancy or snazzy; they're not meant to be. You can write one or 1000. You can make them all the same or each one just a little bit different. It's the voice you use and what you say that makes them personal. A letter is intended to be a communication from one human being to another. And there's precious little of that these days.

When you write a letter:

1. **Don't write the first paragraph first.**
   I see so many people get stuck because they can't get that first thought right. It's better to write the first paragraph last.

2. **Speak directly to your prospect.**
   Imagine you're sitting next to me at a networking event. I've just asked what you do. Tell me, don't sell me. Frame everything from my perspective (hint: using the word "you" will help to achieve this perspective).

3. **Don't get too personal.**
   There is a clear distinction between personal and disrespectful. For example, don't use your prospect's first name unless you actually know them. Besides being presumptive, it's just plain unprofessional.

4. **Use your own voice to speak to your prospect.**
   Speak casually and don't try to impress anyone. Use simple rather than fancy words.

The Look of a Letter

Once a week, usually on a Sunday evening, I actually sit down and go through the week's pile of mail. That's the only time I have to focus my attention on it – and I'm one of the more conscientious ones. I've seen enough offices with piles of unopened mail to know that I'm not the norm.

So, keeping in mind that most people don't ever read their mail, keep in mind that in order to get your message across, you need to focus as much on the graphics of your letter as on the content. For example, if a letter isn't skimmable, if the paragraphs are too thick, the copy too dense, no matter what it says, it may not be read. You could be giving away money, and it wouldn't matter.

Veteran copywriter, Don Hauptman, offers these suggestions:

1. **Don't use a dizzying variety of fonts, type sizes or graphics just because you can.**
    When people open an envelope, they expect to see a letter, with it familiar conventions. The personal communication may be an illusion but it's one that most of us have come to expect.

2. **Write short paragraphs.**
    To avoid a gray wall of type that discourages reading, paragraphs shouldn't be more than 7 lines. A visual and dramatic break can be provided by an occasional paragraph made up of a single sentence line, or even one word.

3. **Use familiar attention devices**
    a. Underscore key words and sentences with a continuous line
    b. Use bullets of any shape to set off an easy-to-read list
    c. Use subheads, set in slightly larger type, to break up the copy
    d. Use inset paragraphs to call attention to an important point.

4. **Handwrite something.**
   People used to be afraid that handwriting anything on a business letter would make it look unprofessional. Now, the opposite is true. Handwriting a PS, or even the salutation on a form letter, lets your prospect know there's a human being behind the computer; it's a sign of life that people desperately need in this era of pseudo-personalized everything

5. **Less is more.**
   One page only, if you can help it. Don't send something that will be eligible for the To Read pile

6. **Always use a P.S.**
   It's the first read (and the most read) element of a letter. Use it to either restate your main point, in case your reader misses it, or to highlight a premium offer or major benefit.

Cheap Direct Mail Tricks

Have you ever done a mailing, been disappointed, then given up on direct mail? Be honest now...

Well I hear "direct mail doesn't work" all the time from clients who don't get the response they expect. But one mailing does not direct mail make. You can't just do something once then abandon the effort when it fails – and it will.

The only way direct mail works is by conducting a campaign. The word implies a commitment to marketing. It's the cumulative effect of direct mail – frequency, not quantity – that produces the results everyone raves about.

Postcards: a Beginner's Direct Mail Campaign

A postcard campaign is the easiest campaign to start with, but that doesn't make it any less effective.

Postcards can be used for many different marketing purposes:

Postcard Introduction – To generate leads, to prompt a recipient to call for more info

Postcard Follow-up – To spark action by prospects who have already received your detailed materials but haven't taken the next step

Postcard Reminder – To remind prospects of your existence and their interest

Postcard Announcement – To convey a quick message about a special offer or sale

Cheap 4/c Postcards

Although many in the design industry regularly use a 4-color postcard with an image to promote their work, I think anyone can do the same, even if your business doesn't have to do with design. Any image that relates to your business will do.

Do-it-Yourself Postcards

I regularly receive hand-made postcards from an illustrator who simply pastes a color-copied image onto a piece of cardboard. There's room for a label and a short message on the other side. It definitely stands out in my pile of mail. But you don't have to be an artist to make your own postcards.

Envelopes

The Cardinal rule of envelope copy according to author, Herschell Gordon Lewis, is this: The only purpose of the carrier envelope, other than keeping its contents from spilling out onto the street, is to get itself opened.

Colored envelopes command attention. So do envelopes with unusual designs and textures. Test your envelope by slipping it into a pile of your mail. Wait a few hours or even a day (i.e. forget about it), then go through your pile. What did you see first? Does your envelope stand out? Would you open it first? If not, what did grab your attention? Can you apply that to your direct mail?

Everyone Loves Lumpy Mail

I recently received a lumpy envelope with a ringing business card holder. It actually rings, like a telephone, until you close it. Now, I'm not sure I'd actually use this; in fact I'm not sure how it's meant to be used. But I was curious to know what was causing the lump and I spent more time on that piece of mail than on any other. These people did the right thing to get me to stop, although they didn't get me to the next step. (With that product, I don't think they could have.) So here's the question: how can you create a lump?

Labels

Labels have become so widely used that they're no longer impersonal, especially on postcards. Try a clear plastic label, which creates the initial impression of an individually addressed envelope. Or make your label stand out by highlighting your prospect's name in a fancy typeface and making it bigger than the address. Don't go wild though. The name has to be legible. Also, labels are the perfect place for clip art. A little icon can quickly grab someone's attention.

The Ultimate Direct Mail Piece: the Thank-You Card

Thank everyone you meet for anything they give, or even merely offer. Do it writing and do it right away.

If you play it right, it can generate all kinds of interesting possibilities. It's such a simple thing to do – too simple perhaps – so very few people do it. I find it interesting to see who takes the time to thank me for a referral. I don't remember who doesn't but I do remember who does.

More Direct Mail Tips

Get into your prospect's head

When you get disappointing results from a marketing effort, you wonder, "Why aren't they calling?" But if you want people to respond, you must think like them.

Before you do any marketing, you must step into your prospect's shoes, imagine their life, imagine their desk. Let's say someone like me is your prospect. When I receive something in the mail from a stranger, here's what I want:

- A short letter, maybe even on a small piece of paper, which tells me in a nutshell what they do and why I should care

- A response vehicle, so that if I'm interested I can easily request more information by returning something or calling an 800 number

- A web site I can go to for more information

- A simple brochure describing the products or services

- Something personal or real, telling me why I'm receiving this. Don't be lazy. Take the extra step and include a short note. Even a post-it is fine.

The Keyhole View

If there's one skill we've perfected, it's that of tuning out. And I don't now about you but I want to throw away as much mail as possible. I don't want to take anything out of an envelope unless I have to. I slit open the envelope, peek inside and if I don't see something interesting, it goes into the trash. That's the keyhole view.

So your job, as a marketer, is to target well enough so that your mail, your offer, and your service is important and needed by your prospect.

Help your recipients cut through their junk to what's really important. Help them say yes to this question: "Does this deserve my valuable time and attention?"

If the answer is no, it's truly not worth their time or yours.

CHAPTER 11 | DOES ADVERTISING EVER WORK?

As consumers, we see advertising everywhere so we may think we understand it. It looks easy and besides, it works on us.

Some companies spend their marketing budget on all manner of advertising without knowing if it's really working. Many don't look for guidance until after they've invested, and perhaps wasted, several hundred (or thousand) dollars with one-shot advertising that yields disappointing, if any, results.

The most recent case was an interior designer who'd been seduced by circulation numbers and talked into placing a one-time display ad in a special semi- annual, Home Design supplement to The New York Times Magazine. When the ad came out, her phone rang, all right, but it was vendor after vendor trying to sell her something.

What is Advertising?

Often people use the word advertising when they mean marketing, and vice versa. So before we launch into a discussion of either, let's define our terms. Marketing is the umbrella; it's everything you do to promote your business, including publicity, direct mail, networking and, of course, advertising.

Advertising is when you pay for exposure to a certain market by purchasing space where they are likely to see your message.

Publicity (sometimes known as free advertising) is when the media give you exposure, in the form of a profile or review of you and your work, or by citing you as an expert.

When it comes to advertising, you control the message; when you get publicity, they do. There are advantages to both. But as a marketer, it's important to keep in mind that most of us by now are very sophisticated consumers. Your prospects are hip to advertising ploys and wary of the messages that bombard them day and night. On the other hand, as savvy as they may be, those messages can be very confusing and they often don't know if what they're seeing is an ad, an article or something entirely different.

It won't be news when you hear me say that advertising, like all marketing, doesn't work unless you have a carefully thought-out plan and unless you make a long-term commitment to the process. Don't indulge in the haphazard stuff. You'll only be disappointed.

Does Advertising Work?

Well, advertising can work, but it's neither magic nor immediate. Have you heard this joke: I know my advertising is 50% successful, I just don't know which 50%. It's not a joke. Unless you're running direct response ads (like infomercials that encourage people to send money or "click to buy now"), it's near impossible to measure the effect of advertising.

The way advertising works (and all marketing, for that matter) is through repetition. You gain your market's confidence through high visibility and the consistent reinforcement of your marketing message. The messages work as triggers, to remind your prospect that they are interested in your services and products. It has to sink in, below the surface, so that when your prospect has a need, your name, your logo, your message comes to mind.

So the first rule is this: once is not enough. In fact, once is a waste. The chances that your prospect will just happen to see your ad the one time you just happen to advertise is very slim. You have to start small, go slowly, and give it a chance, which means you must run your ad at least six times, or over the course of six months. During that time you can change a word here or there to test its effect on response. Or test three versions of one ad in three different media and see if the differences affect response. Using this strategy, you'll be able to track results, and you'll have time to get a sense of which ad is more effective.

Isn't Advertising Expensive?

Many businesses fail because they don't spend enough money on advertising; others fail because they spend too much, or buy inappropriate ad space. The cost of advertising is measured not in dollars but in response. If you buy an expensive ad and lots of people respond to it, then it wasn't expensive at all. And likewise, the fact that you get a great deal becomes irrelevant if no one sees your ad.

The expensive ads aren't even necessarily the most effective. For example, a classified ad in the back of a neighborhood paper can be more effective – and cheaper – than a snazzy, 4-color display ad in a national magazine.

But size is only one of the issues to consider. Another is the quality of the ad itself: what it looks like, what it says, how the type is laid out. According to Jay Conrad Levinson, author of the Guerilla Marketing series, "Far more people will see your ad than will see you or your place of business, so their opinion will be shaped by your ad."

Unless you want your ad to look like all the other ones, don't let the ad salesperson design your ad or write your copy. They'll offer to do it because they want to make it easy for you to advertise.

If you're going to advertise, do it right. Spend the money to make it look good. Hire a professional to write the copy and to design the layout. This investment will payoff in the long run.

Where Should I Place my Ads?

Be proactive, be decisive, and be creative in your media buy. Put yourself in your prospect's shoes and imagine his or her moment of need. You know your customers. What are his resources? What is the easiest thing for her to do? Go the Yellow Pages? Call a colleague for a referral? Check to see what's floating at the top of the email inbox? Look in a paper file they may be keeping just for moments like these? If you don't know, or if you want more concrete answers, don't hesitate to ask. They'll tell you.

Then, survey the competition: where do they advertise? Or do they? If they don't, there may be a reason for that.

If you're considering buying space in a magazine that reaches your target audience, review several consecutive issues of that magazine. Chances are that if you see repeated ads for products or services that your target audience is likely to buy, you're on the right track. Before signing a contract, interview other advertisers, maybe even a few former advertisers.

And don't just advertise in the media who sales reps are pushy and persistent with you. You must research your market's buying habits and make the best choices for your business.

CHAPTER 12 | FITTING FOLLOW UP INTO YOUR LIFE

After a Mailing

So you did it! It sat for weeks (or months) buried at the bottom of a pile on your desk, but you finally made yourself finish that self promotion mailing. You got the list together. You input the names into your database. You hired a few kids to label and stamp and you got it out the door.

Now what? Are you sitting by the phone waiting for the flood of new projects to come pouring in? Are you relieved because you think you've gotten your marketing out of the way for a while?

Think again. I've said it once and I'll say it again: self promotion is an ongoing process, a constant in every growing and thriving business, and it must be integrated into your day-to-day activities. To free your business from the feast or famine cycle, you have to surrender your shotgun marketing efforts. The real marketing happens through consistency, by keeping in touch with your market over a long period of time so that, when they have a need, your name comes quickly to mind and your number is easy to find.

Don't Worry About Response

Ideally, every marketing effort gets some on your list to respond or buy. Standard marketing experts say that 1-3% response to a direct mailing is above average, but that percentage is based on corporate monoliths mailing millions or, at the very least, hundreds of thousands. When mailing 100, or even 1000, 3% isn't so great. It's probably not nearly enough to keep your business running.

But what if response isn't everything? What if it's just a piece of the puzzle? Then, whether you have a 1% or a 15% return on a mailing means nothing until you know what that means to long-range, bottom-line profit results – beyond response.

Keep on Marketing

So after a mailing, get busy working on an idea for the next marketing effort. Sit down and strategize your follow up calls. Or reserve a place at a seminar. Whatever you do, keep on marketing. Actually, it doesn't really matter what you do, as long as you do something. Putting the word out, in whatever way, inevitably brings people toward you, increasing your odds of doing more business.

Don't freak out during follow up

Don't you hate it when a prospect calls with a (supposedly) urgent need for your services? You drop everything to put together a proposal, begin to clear your schedule to make room for this new project, and then you wait. When you don't hear back, you call to follow up and they say they haven't had time to look at your proposal yet. You wait some more and, though you dread it, you call again. Or maybe you don't, figuring that they'd call you if they were interested. In any case, you never hear from them again.

This happens all the time – not just to you – and there's little you can do about it. Here's what it may look like from your prospect's perspective: on the day they called, this project was at the top of their list; the next day, something else came along which took priority and then kept pushing the project further and further away, until it was on a permanent back burner. They never bothered to let you know, probably because they didn't have time. Or, more likely, they got caught up in their own world, unaware that you were waiting.

Reality Check

The reality is you can't control your prospects. What you can control, however, is how you spend your time. You decide how vigorously you want to pursue each project and how much time you can afford to devote to each prospect. To do that, you have to rate your prospects and prioritize your efforts toward them. The Client Fitness Checklist on page 97 can help.

Follow Up Calls: Should You or Shouldn't You?

Theses days, people rarely return phone calls. It's unprofessional but it's reality. So now, more than ever, it's up to you to follow up.

For qualified leads (i.e. hot prospects and especially those who've contacted you), follow up calls are a must. Make the call approximately one week after your information is sent out, on any day but Monday. For cold prospects (i.e. people who don't know you), follow up calls are also a must – if you want to work with those prospects, that is. It's unrealistic to think that you could call all recipients of a big mailing; but you could certainly make calls to your A list – i.e. your best prospects. Chances are they got your mail and it's in a pile somewhere. Your phone call will resurrect your material from that pile and, because timing is everything in marketing, possibly provide the final push needed to get the project on track.

Case Study

John Rocha of Rocha & Associates sends small, greeting card-size mailers to names culled from trade magazines and trade show directories. The mailer says, "Drop us a dime" and includes 2 actual dimes. Rocha sends out less than 50 pieces at a time, which makes follow up calls to each recipient manageable. His prospect usually claims not to have seen the mailing at first, but when he mentions the dimes, his prospect always remembers. When Rocha isn't able to reach his target on the phone he follows up with a letter and then continues to keep in touch. *"It's just a question of reaching them at the right time,"* says Rocha, who spends 5% of gross sales on marketing and estimates a 5-10% sale rate. *"We know it's working by the work that we get. The mailings are noticeably profitable. We could track a sale back to an actual mailing, but we don't. Part of the success is establishing the relationship and you need to contact someone five or six times before that's achieved."*

A Primer of Follow Up Lingo

If you never know what to say, these phrases might help. Keep them handy.

For follow up letters:

- **Begin with:**
  "Thanks for speaking to me (or meeting with me). I know your time is valuable."

- **Recap with:**
  "As we discussed…"

- **End with:**
  "I look forward to continuing our conversation."

- **Always include a call to action, such as:**
  - Call me with any questions
  - Call me to continue this conversation
  - Let me know if I can be of any help.

For follow up phone calls:

"We haven't spoken in a while and I wanted to check in and see if anything has changed with…"

"Perhaps you are in a better position than when we first spoke to use our services?"

"I was wondering if you are still planning to go forward with the project we discussed."

What They Say	What You Hear	What They Mean	What You Do
I have a project. I need a proposal.	They want me	They're gathering info on potential candidates	Send your info. Follow up to confirm they got it.
I'm sure it's here somewhere. I haven't had time to look at it yet	They don't want me	Other things have come up and the project isn't quite as urgent	Ask when to call back
I've looked over your materials and they look interesting, but we haven't yet decided what direction to take. We'll be in touch.	They don't like it. Or they chose someone else	They're still strategizing	Ask when they'll be making a decision
The project is on hold. We'll be in touch	They chose someone else.	They're busy with other things or maybe they did choose someone else. It's not the end of the world.	Keep in touch every few months by email, mail and phone.

Client Fitness Checklist

You can't follow up with everyone, and the good news is, you don't have to. But in order to decide whom to pursue and whom to let go, you have to determine their value to you – qualify them, in marketing lingo. The big question is: is there a fit? Don't be so eager to get a project that you fail to consider a prospect's fitness for you. Here is a checklist of questions to ask yourself about each prospect that will help you assign a rating: A, B, C or Hot, Warm, Cold, whatever labels work for you.

Business Potential
1. Why aren't they still working with their previous vendor?
2. Do they have future needs? Immediate needs?
3. Is there potential for ongoing business?

The Decision-Making Process
1. Is your contact the decision maker?
2. Are there several layers of bureaucracy to deal with?
3. Can they afford you?
4. Can they pay a percentage up front?

Personality/Working Style
1. Does your contact respect your time and labor?
2. Do they require a lot of hand-holding?
3. Do they understand that you have other clients?
4. Do they buy based solely on price? Quality? Both?
5. Do they respect your professional boundaries?
6. Do they do business honestly and with integrity?
7. Do you feel comfortable with them?

Your fitness for them
1. Does this project fit into your specialty?
2. Could you refer someone who would be a better fit?
3. Do they require more time than you have available?

Once you've given each prospect a rating, determine your strategy. Here's a sample rating system and strategy:

*   **Hot:** Has an immediate need. Follow up right away.

*   **Warm:** Will have a need soon. Ask how they want you to follow up.

*   **Cool:** May have future needs. Keep on the mailing list and contact quarterly.

*   **Cold:** Worth one call to see that they received information. Otherwise, let them come to you.

CHAPTER 13 | YOU? A PUBLISHER?

Did you know that newsletters have a 400% higher readership than standard promotional materials? It's true. At the same time, there is no end in sight to information overload. People are increasingly selective about what they spend their time actually reading. Aren't you? The Internet is supposed to help but it doesn't. It just adds to the deluge!

Dealing with Information Overload

According to an article in DM Magazine, it is not more information that people desire. What they want is relevant information edited to meet their needs and dispensed at the appropriate time to gain their attention and action. Customers seek to expand control over their environment and to separate the relevant from the noise.

To Publish or Not to Publish

You are multi-talented and creative in your business. You offer a variety of services and products that your customers need. But how do you communicate the range and breadth of your capabilities without boring or overwhelming your prospects? You rarely have their attention for long enough to elaborate on even one aspect of your work, much less everything you do.

Wouldn't it be ideal if you could sit with each client a few times a year to describe one more aspect of your business? Soon enough, they would know a lot about you and would, as a result, be able to use (and refer) more of your services. Of course, this is logistically impossible.

However, a promotional newsletter – whether email or printed – can have this effect. It allows information to come through in small, bite-size pieces, each time allowing them to add to what they already know about you. It can be the perfect vehicle to increase awareness about your services and products, while at the same time providing information that is of value to them.

So if you are thinking about publishing a newsletter, the question to ask yourself is this: How can you create something short but valuable to your market, so much that it stands out from the rest of the clutter?

Newsletter as Marketing Tool

Ten Reasons to publish a newsletter (printed or electronic)

1. It can provide an informative, soft-sell introduction to prospects.

2. It can provide them with information they can use, rather than fluff about you.

3. It can keep you in touch on a regular basis, without being perceived as a pest.

4. It can keep your customers up-to-date on your services and products.

5. It can remind prospects, past clients and colleagues that you exist. And may motivate them to contact you.

6. It can demonstrate your expertise in a field.

7. It can educate them when they have no time to educate themselves.

8. It can provide an opportunity or forum for you to explain complicated products, services or offers, which is especially helpful if your business is not familiar.

9. It can trigger more sales by providing tips on how to use your products/services.

10. It can really enhance your credibility

Promotional vs. Subscription

First of all, let's define our terms. I'm not talking about a paid subscription newsletter. I'm talking about a promotional newsletter that you send, at no charge, to your prospects and clients in an effort to keep your name in front of them. With a promotional newsletter, you have more freedom. You can send it out on an irregular basis. You have no commitment to anyone but yourself, and generally few expectations from your recipients.

Promoting Yourself in a Newsletter

A promotional newsletter is not a brochure, catalogue or sales letter. While it is an opportunity to market yourself, your own self promotion should not be the focus of the content. If it is, I guarantee, your newsletter will not be read. A promotional newsletter can include more self promotion than a subscription newsletter, but it should be done subtly and, ideally, via an informational format.

Show, don't tell. Educate and entertain your readers. Demonstrate your expertise. Cover topics that your clients may not know you know about. Give examples of projects you've worked on. Tell success stories. Let your newsletter show off your talents and capabilities, especially if what you do can actually be conveyed in this medium, (i.e. graphic design, illustration, writing).

How to Use Your Newsletter

Though I just said a newsletter isn't a brochure, it can in fact double as one, and, in doing so, have a much greater impact. Here are few ways to use a promotional newsletter.

1. **Use it like a brochure.**
    When someone calls asking for information, you can send a newsletter with a cover letter highlighting only the services that prospect would find most interesting.

2. **Use it like a press release.**
    The media is always looking for information that is of value to their readers. Almost all of the publicity I've garnered has been a result of reporters reprinting something they found useful in my newsletter. Sometimes, they even pay a reprint fee. That's found money!

3. **Use it to gather information about the needs of your prospects and clients.**
    Encourage response through surveys or by asking pointed questions to which they can simply click "reply" to answer.

So You've Decided to Publish a Newsletter

Some newsletter do's:

1. **Educate.**
    Provide information that's relevant, noteworthy and beneficial. Keep articles short, concise, focused and chock-full of practical information.

2. **Show what you know and use yourself as an example.**
    This simultaneously illustrates the point you're trying to make and gives more details about what you do, just in case...

3. **Let them get to know you.**
    Use the opportunity to make your prospects and clients connoisseurs of your product or services. This strengthens ties and fosters future sales. Teach them how to distinguish between high and low quality in your industry, among your colleagues and your competition. Examples: printers can talk about paper quality, designers can discuss the importance of good design, etc.

4. Make them feel special.
   Give them sneak previews, or offer customer-only specials or prices.

5. **Create a dialogue between you and your readers.**
   While you can use a newsletter to talk to them, you can create ways to listen to them as well. Encourage their feedback and suggestions.

Frequency

Don't get yourself in over your head. Don't promise a weekly publication if you've never done this before. Start with a Premier Issue. Call it an "occasional newsletter" so no one is sitting around waiting for the next one. Then, see how it goes, if it fits into your day-to-day or month-to-month. If you decide to make it a regular thing, start with quarterly. From there you can slowly increase your frequency to no more often than monthly. That's really plenty. As for length, if it's a printed piece, two pages is a good starting place – that's two sides of one page. You can slowly increase the quantity of information as you go along. If it's email, the shorter the better.

What about those Boilerplate Newsletters?

As you probably know, there are companies who sell generic newsletters, onto which you can have your name printed. Then you send it out to everyone on your mailing list. This is easy, requires very little effort on your part and, as a result, is a pretty boring marketing effort. Because companies who publish these newsletters sell them to large markets, (mostly lawyers, accountants and other professionals) they have to be fairly generic, which by definition makes them boring. Personally, I don't like them. The information always seems old, and if it's not fresh, no one will take the time to read it.

What about a Mini Newsletter?

If creating a newsletter seems like too much work, a Tip Sheet is the solution for you. A Tip Sheet is a short list of handy tips that you offer to your clients, a sample of your expertise.

For example, I could easily make a tip sheet out of 10 Reasons to Publish a Newsletter. I'd just add my byline, (one or two lines about who I am, what I do and how people can contact me). Have it copied onto card stock and send it out as a postcard.

Printing and Mailing

Look for a printer who's flexible, maybe even someone who'd be willing to do the printing in exchange for use of the newsletter for their own promotional efforts. Two-color is fine. Don't waste money on four colors unless you've got money to burn.

Design it to be a self mailer (i.e. make a place for the label and stamp), so that you don't need an envelope, which costs you more and decreases your odds of getting it opened.

Mail first class, unless you're mailing thousands

Newsletter Worksheet

If you don't know what to put in your newsletter, here are some guidelines for creating content.

- Answer the question "what do you do" in 25 words.

- List 3 areas of expertise that you have.

- List any products or services you are preparing to offer.

- Describe one complicated aspect of your business that prospects sometimes have trouble understanding.

- Write three tips relating to your business that your clients would find useful.

- List the publications you think they need to read but may not be getting to. Now, turn this information into newsletter content.

The Elements of a Newsletter

Content: where does it come from?

First of all, know that you have a choice. Just because you've decided to put out a newsletter doesn't mean you have to write the thing. Consider using your newsletter to digest for your market the information they probably aren't getting to, like books, magazines or other newsletters. To find out what those materials are, simply ask.

You can also use your newsletter to voice your thoughts, offering your unique perspective on the industry. Both approaches are valid and of value to your prospects. Decide which way to go based on what you enjoy and the amount of real time you can devote to this project.

Ideas for Original Material

The worksheet will help you develop the content for your newsletter. Here are some guidelines:

- **Quick Tips.**
  People just love quick tips, especially bulleted or in list form, which makes them especially easy to read. "Ten Things You Should Know" or "Seven Easy Ways to…" And there's no rule about how many tips to give.

- **Your perspective.**
  Write an article presenting your perspective on an industry trend, like an Op-Ed piece.

- **Promote your clients.**
  Tell success stories of projects you've worked on. Or write a profile of a client. Make sure you include their contact info so they can be reached. If you don't want to do all that work, you

can offer your client the opportunity to write something. Then give them a stack to mail to their clients, which only increases your exposure.

If You Use Unoriginal Material

- **Give resources.**
  Gather information from sources you find useful and request permission to reprint it in your publication.

- **Check facts.**
  Typographical and factual errors are a mark of carelessness and unreliability. If you provide resources, call all phone numbers to make sure they're current and in working order.

Tone

The tone you set with your choice of language, color and typestyle can say a lot about your business. You can probably tell from my conversational tone that my marketing perspective is also down-to-earth and jargon-free. Don't make yours feel official and stilted unless you are that way. Let your newsletter be a reflection of you; let it show who you are and what you know.

The Visuals

For an email newsletter, I highly recommend using an email marketing service because they will provide a visually appealing template that reflects your "brand identity." All you do is type in the text. We use (and love) www.myemmamail.com (and if you mention Marketing Mentor, you get a 20% discount).

CHAPTER 14 | THE DOABLE MARKETING PLAN

How many times have you wanted to create a marketing plan…but just didn't take the time to sit down and do it? Or maybe you've started the process but never finished it? The truth is you don't have to have a plan. It is possible to run, and even grow, your business without one – most people do.

However, without a plan, your marketing is probably haphazard, scattered and slipshod. A marketing opportunity pops up, maybe an ad in a special section of the local paper or a trade show you weren't planning to exhibit at, and you jump at it because you've been meaning to do some marketing.

So you create that ad or slap together a promo piece to hand out at your booth. But because it's the last minute, you don't have the time to proof-read, so there are a few typographical errors, or maybe you forget to put your phone number on it. But at least it's done – and you go back to doing your work and wait for the new clients to come knocking on your door, which could happen, I suppose. That's one option.

If, on the other hand, you have a marketing plan into which you fit that ad or trade show because it aligns with the strategy you have in place, you can make time for the necessary preparation, execution and follow through in a methodical way. A marketing plan doesn't have to be an overwhelming task – a 100 page manuscript that you slave over and then put on your shelf to gather dust; it can fit on one page. It can be simple to write and easy to use. Anyone, with or without marketing experience, can create one.

Do whatever it takes to step away from your workaday life to plan the short-term and long-term future of your business. One morning every month, close your office door or go out for breakfast, alone or with a colleague, to focus on planning for the future of your business. If taking time out of your workday seems impossible, see if you can spend one weekend morning per month on it. Because if you don't, you'll be chasing your business from behind, rather than being the driving force behind it.

What's a Marketing Plan?

Basic Definitions

Now, perhaps you are reluctant to create a marketing plan because you're not exactly sure what it is or how it differs from a business plan. They both sound pretty corporate, a standard formula you're supposed to follow (which you don't know), and it probably takes a lot of time (which you don't have).

Some plans are like that but yours doesn't have to be. A business plan is generally a very complex document that you create in order to get financing, such as a loan from a bank. It forces you to think through many of the issues you may not take the time to consider otherwise, and it shows lenders that you are serious. So, even if you're not looking for financing, creating a business plan is an excellent exercise. But many people don't have time for business exercises. I know I don't.

A marketing plan is different. It's for you; it's not for anyone else. It never really becomes a finished document because it is always in process. You build your business in the creating and the working of the plan.

Your plan doesn't have to be more than one page, and there is no standard format for it. I have one client who's afraid of putting her marketing plan in a drawer and forgetting about it so hers is on an oversized calendar on the wall of her office. This way she always sees it and is reminded of what she's doing – or supposed to be doing.

I like to think of marketing plans in the plural. You won't create one plan once and for all. I hope you will create a different plan for every objective you have, so that maybe you'll be working two or three plans simultaneously. But that's a bit advanced. Let's just start with one and then expand from there.

A Marketing Plan is a Structure

It is a structure that you create and within which you work toward your goals. A marketing plan is your map to more business – a set of steps that will lead you toward a specific objective you have set for yourself.

Your plan can have a narrow focus and a finite timetable with objectives such as *I want to earn $100,000 per year, I want to create a press kit,* or *I want to introduce myself to a new market.* It can include a carefully chosen market and a timetable of when and how to complete the steps. Or, your plan can be more open, consisting of tools that are self-driven, such as a monthly email newsletter, quarterly phone calls or a bi-monthly postcard – any consistent vehicle that supports the ongoing development of your business relationships and works to avoid the feast or famine syndrome.

Do I Have a Plan?

You have to be wondering. In fact, there are a few different kinds of plans that work for me. For the ongoing marketing of my business, here it is in a nutshell: networking is a major element in my plan. I attend 1-2 events per month because it's important to meet people, to take time to get to know them and to let them know me. I then use my email newsletter to promote the Marketing Mentor program and workshops to prospects, contacts, subscribers and clients – everyone who knows me.

For very specific objectives, I use the standard one-page marketing plan format to organize the tasks.

My big picture plan is less concrete. It is set up as a list of goals (personal and business) that I'd like to reach. I keep the list posted on my bulletin board so I don't forget what I'm aiming toward. Every 6 months or so, I evaluate and revise them, add to them, subtract from them. That's my plan.

Marketing Plan = Freedom

Since you design your own plan, you have the freedom to choose only those things you want to do and to change the steps according to the evolution of your priorities. Your marketing plan is not a weapon; it's designed to help you, not hurt you. It is as unique and individual as you are and can be as flexible as you need it to be. It can save you time, energy and money – if you let it.

How to Create Your One Page Marketing Plan

1. **Determine what you want.**

   Ideally, you'll have more than one marketing plan and each one will be designed to achieve a specific objective. Here are some examples of objectives: to get 3 new projects, to get an article in the paper, to get one monthly retainer client. For the purpose of this exercise, let's say you are a copywriter and your objective is to introduce yourself to a new market and to get one new project in one month.

2. **Choose your market and find a list.**

   Market: direct mail agencies, ad agencies and design studios.
   List source: trade publications and local association directories

3. **List the marketing tools you will use.**

   Tools: research phone calls, introductory letter/packet, follow up phone calls, networking meetings, promotional follow up postcard

4. **Determine how much time and money are available to you.** Time: 3 hours per week. Money: $1,000.

5. **Break down your plan into logical, manageable (i.e. small) steps.** Determine which tools you will use and in what order.
   - Week 1: Gather the information to create a list of 20 prospects.
   - Week 2: Write an introductory letter. Have someone proofread it.
   - Week 3: Call first 10 companies for contact name
   - Week 4: Send first batch of letters
   - Week 5: Follow up calls to the first batch
   - Week 6: Call second 10 companies for contact name
   - Week 7: Send second batch of 10 letters
   - Week 8: Follow up calls to second batch
   - Week 9: Evaluate plan so far and make any necessary changes

Your one page marketing plan
- Step 1: objective
- Step 2: Target Market and list source
- Step 3: Marketing tools
- Step 4: Time and money budgets
- Step 5: Timetable for tasks
- Week 1
- Week 2
- Week 3
- Week 4
- Week 5
- Week 6
- Week 7
- Week 8

CHAPTER 15 | DO IT YOURSELF PUBLIC RELATIONS

The power of the media

When I started my business in 1988, I had no idea what I was doing. My idea was to be a professional organizer, so I joined the newly formed New York chapter of the National Association of Professional Organizers.

At the same time, I had friends – actors, musicians and artists – who were asking me to help them with what turned out to be self promotion, though at the time I had no idea that's what I was doing.

So when, at a NAPO meeting, I met a woman who said she was writing a story on organizers for New York Magazine and asked me for names of people I'd worked with, I didn't think much if it and gave her phone numbers for my two or three only clients.

The blurb she ended up writing about me said I was an organizer who also did self promotion. My phone didn't stop ringing for months!

All those years ago, I knew nothing about publicity and certainly wasn't trying to get any. But I was in the right place at the right time and, of all the organizers this woman interviewed, I was different from the others because of the self promotion angle which made me desirable for inclusion.

As a result of that small paragraph of publicity I was able to quit the part-time gigs I'd arranged and devote myself full time to what evolved into Marketing Mentor. Incredibly, I sometimes still get calls from that article!

How Publicity Really Works

The myth of free publicity

Yes, it's essentially free advertising and, yes, it's better than any paid ad because it appears in an objective, editorial environment and because people are incredibly impressed by the printed word. But it's not free, by any stretch of the imagination; it requires a very heavy investment of time, sometimes money, and very selective targeting.

Whenever I get a call from a reporter who wants to include me or an excerpt from one of my articles or books in a publication, I start imagining the flood of phone calls that will be coming my way. Despite my New York Magazine experience, however, it rarely happens that way. In fact, since then, the effect of publicity has been much slower, which, I've discovered, is more typical.

Publicity is a process, and, like all valuable marketing tools, it takes time. Publicity is cumulative; momentum gathers. People start to see your name around. They don't remember where they saw it, but each time, they are reminded of their interest in you, your services and products.

But publicity doesn't promise any actual clients. Only a cohesive, consistent marketing plan with a variety of tools can do that. Publicity is just one tool. Sometimes it motivates people to call, especially if the timing is right. But if they're not in their moment of need, they'll either clip the article and save it (or lose it) or they'll make a mental note and let it go by, perhaps imagining they'll see it again somewhere.

If they've heard of you before, because you made a cold call last month or met them at a trade show, for example, then publicity supports and reinforces your message. It's just another way to get your name across their desk.

Put Yourself in Their Shoes

The press is a group of people suffering from intense information overload. They are barraged every day; expensive media kits don't impress them and gifts and gimmicks don't endear them to you. They're on the lookout for real, valuable information that their readers can use. If you want coverage, that is what you must provide.

Create relationships with writers and editors in the same way that you create relationships with prospects. Again, more is not better. Don't do a mass mailing of your press release and then sit back and wait for the press coverage to roll in. Your time and resources are better used if you choose 10 or 25 carefully targeted publications for your release, then customize each one for the style of each publication.

Position yourself as someone they can count on for help. Writers and editors have serious deadlines that are not easy to meet. Sometimes stories fall through at the last minute or subjects turn out to be worthless and they need material, so one of their basic needs is a quick response from their resources. That means returning phone calls immediately, for example, or sending a photo right away. Having a reliable source is of utmost importance to them. Be that and you're golden.

What's Fresh About You?

The lifeblood of the media is anything new and different. Your objective is to show the media what's different about you. Editors can't recycle the same old ideas and tips issue after issue so they're always on the lookout for something "fresh". For example, because my email newsletter is one of my most vital marketing tools, (and publicity is one of my most effective), one of my goals is to come up with ideas that are "fresh." If you want publicity, that's what you've got to give them.

But how do you figure out what's fresh about your business? And what if you think there isn't really anything fresh about you? Impossible, I say. Every person is different, therefore every business is different. If you have a hard time coming up with your uniqueness, here's a tool that can help you.

Following is an excerpt from "66 Ways to Make You or Your Business Newsworthy," by Marcia Yudkin, author of "Six Steps to Free Publicity."

- Offer surprising facts tied to your business
- Do a survey and publish the results
- Conduct business in an unusual setting (like the zoo)

Note: I've just given Marcia's book a plug, which just might motivate many of you to buy a copy. It's that simple.

13 Tips for Getting an Editor's Attention

Choosing editors, writers and publications:

1. **Study the publications prior to sending information.**
   Each release should be tailored to each publication for greater impact.

2. **Read bylines, know who's who, and follow the writers who follow your field.**
   Watch which ones cover business topics, which ones are writing articles in which you could have been featured. They're the ones to write to. Always be adding to your press list. Be on the lookout for new publications that might be receptive to what you have to say.

3. **Get the right name and spell it right.**
   Make sure your press list is up to date. There are constant changes which aren't immediately apparent on a web site or on the masthead so be sure to call the publication to find out who to contact.

Getting the right info to them:

4. **Don't overwhelm them with piles of paper.**

   If you're sending a press kit, be selective and consider which press clippings would mean the most to that particular writer. Some publications will walk away if you have been overexposed, believing the story has been done to death. Others take a lot of coverage as proof of your value to readers. Try to find out which camp your key media contacts fit into.

5. **Get to the point.**

   Whether you fax, email or send it via snail mail, write a simple, a one page letter or news release and put the key information in the first paragraph, using the others to elaborate with details.

6. **Jot a note in the margin of a release.**

   Use the editor's name – but only if you've had contact with them and draw an arrow to highlight what might be of special interest to that editor's particular audience.

7. **Give them art:**

   Line drawings, b/w or color photos, bars and graphs, they need it.

Nurturing your press relationships

8. **Always thank an editor or reporter**

   for including you in a piece and let them know what kind of response you've received.

9. **Keep in touch on a regular basis.**

   Research indicates that editors are more receptive to information they get regularly from the same company. Not that they'll always use it, but consistency keeps your name in front of them in a positive way.

10. **Get on the media's agenda.**
    They are more likely to use your information if you address the timely topics that they are reporting on.

11. **Target the publication your prospects read consistently**
    so they see your name again and again, and it becomes familiar to them.

12. **Send information to each publication in their style**
    and they're more likely to use it. It cuts down on their work.

13. **In a nutshell, you must:**
    Pitch to the right person, come up with an interesting angle, be honest about the news value of your information.

Seven Kinds of Publicity

1. **Being included in a resource list.**
   Newsletters, book, and magazine articles sometimes list resources and if you can find the ones you fit into and get listed, your prospect has to do no work besides dialing your number, which is why I think this is most valuable.

2. **A calendar listing for an event you either sponsor or are involved in.** When we put on marketing workshops, we send a blurb to local business papers. Not only have I had inquiries about the workshop, but often I get inquiries from people who want to know more about the business. This type of publicity raises curiosity about your business and, again, your phone number is right there.

3. **Tips on your topic.**
   This is one of the easiest ways to get publicity because you're providing a publication with material that doesn't need any work beyond a bit of editing. If it's fresh or useful, they'll pick

it up. And you can often get your address and phone number included, which is essential, but you usually have to ask.

4. **An article or profile on your company.**
   For obvious reasons, this can be very valuable. The potential downside is that you have no control over what is written and a writer's goal is rarely to show you in the best light. But if you do like the final version, you may be able to use the piece in place of a brochure, with the added value of an objective recommendation.

5. **Being cited as an expert within the context of an article.**
   Though this sometimes doesn't generate more than a few inquiries (depending on the article, of course), this kind of publicity bestows high credibility and is very impressive when copied and sent out as part of your marketing package.

6. **An article written by you.**
   This is an opportunity to show what you know. However, unless you're a writer or are prepared to hire someone to ghostwrite an article for you, don't waste your time on this. If you do feel comfortable doing the writing, begin by sending a query letter with a few article ideas. Don't write the article first. Let the editor choose the idea he/she likes best. You may get paid for this, but at the beginning, don't expect to. Just make sure you negotiate for a byline that includes your phone number and web site.

7. **Letter to the editor.**
   Prospects generally don't act on what they read in these letters but they're valuable to write, can help you crystallize ideas, and can sometimes turn into a full-fledged article. If you are moved by something, write a letter!

When thinking about publicity, be clear about the kind of coverage you want and what kind each writer, editor or publication can offer.

All publicity is valuable – from other people's email newsletters to big, national consumer publications – because you never know who is reading what. Just keep in mind that, looking for stories and useful information, the press reads everything. Even coverage in *The Art of Self Promotion Newsletter* can garner bigger and better coverage, as it did for Randy Rosler of IntroKnocks when I featured his business in an issue of the newsletter.

Somehow, one of the editors at Gannett Publications got a hold of it (someone who wasn't even on my press list), and he ended up doing a big spread on Randy's business in a Long Island business paper. You just never know!

And don't be afraid to ask to have your phone number included. It could mean the difference between a drip and a flood of phone calls!

For more on getting publicity, read "Public Relations for Dummies," which I co-authored with Eric Yaverbaum and Bob Bly.

CHAPTER 16 | YOU PROBABLY DON'T NEED A BROCHURE

What is a Brochure?

A brochure is simply a way to tell your prospects the basic facts of your business. It is used to whet their appetite.

Sometimes, people confuse a brochure and a catalog, using the terms interchangeably. One difference, according to some customers, is that a catalog is used mainly for products, showcasing everything available. So, for example, a brochure could precede a request for a catalog. Or a brochure can pick up where an introductory letter leaves off.

You May Not Need a Brochure

The creation of a brochure can be an expensive process and, depending on your business, may be unnecessary. Most brochures are never read. These days, people rarely have time to read even the things they are required to read, much less that which comes unsolicited in the mail.

The main reason your prospect wants to see your brochure is to get a sense of the company she's considering doing business with. But there are other ways to give your prospect the information she needs if you can't afford the time or money necessary to create a brochure. Alternatives include letters, web sites, blogs, flyers, newsletters and an active mailing or emailing schedule – all of which offer flexibility and are considerably more cost-efficient.

So, Do You Need a Brochure?

You'll have to decide for yourself. But keep in mind that the quality of any promotional piece is associated with the perceived image of the company it represents. So no matter what that promo piece is, make it the best it can be.

So You've Decided to do a Brochure

A brochure can be the perfect marketing tool for your business. Its mere presence can communicate a very strong message. If, for example, your brochure is of the 4-color, glossy variety, it conveys one message. If it's a homespun 3-fold, another message is conveyed. Neither is better than the other, just different.

Here's a tip: your brochure must be a true representation of your company. You can print anything you want but it's bad business to create an impression that isn't true to you and your company. If you're homespun, be proud of it and say so. Not everyone is impressed by a big company.

A brochure can be very impressive and has the power to impart a feeling of stability and reliability. It can legitimize your company, assuring prospects that your business is solid. For service-oriented companies especially, when there is no tangible product to show, the value of a brochure is in its substance. Likewise, product-oriented companies generally need a brochure or catalog to showcase their offerings.

Should you do it yourself?

You probably think you can. With computers and the variety of desktop publishing programs available, it seems easy to create your own brochure, but it's usually not as easy as it looks. If you're busy running and promoting your business, you probably won't be able to give your best attention to the creation of your promotional piece, which is essential. More importantly, experts (like graphic designers and copywriters) bring a valuable perspective to the process, ensuring the best end result.

But money's always an issue. The cost of a brochure depends on the impression you want to convey and how much that impression costs. It can cost almost nothing to do a letter and a fact sheet and put it in a nice folder, which can be perfectly adequate. On the other hand, you could hire a designer and a copywriter and have it printed, which will cost more but is also likely to create a very powerful and professional impression. It all depends on how important that impression is to your prospects. Some need to be impressed first. The question is: do yours?

I highly recommend that you don't do this alone. There are many kinds of assistance available. You could hire a marketing consultant who would be responsible for creating the concept and executing it, from copy and content through design, to the printed piece. This option is good if you have some money and no time.

You could also hire a design firm to coordinate the project and they should hire a copywriter. If they don't, beware, some designers are good marketers and some can write but very few people can do both well.

If you have a limited budget for your brochure, think about what you can do yourself. I don't recommend that you write the copy yourself because, although you certainly know your business better than anyone, you need the objectivity of an outsider to describe your business to your prospects. Hire a copywriter to write from scratch or, at the very least, have a copywriter or marketing consultant edit and critique your copy.

Don't rush. I've seen too many cases where people are eager to get the brochure done and don't want to spend any time extra time or money. Inevitably, the result is that, after they've invested a great deal, they fail to get their message across and the brochures are unusable. Don't let this happen to you. There are many options available. Choose the one that's right for you.

Creating your Promotional Piece

- **Research**

  Collect promotional materials from everywhere – especially your competition – and study them from an objective perspective. Look for what you like. What do you find easy to read? What do you find difficult to read? What design elements appeal to you?

  Also, ask your clients what they think of your ideas. Ask what they're looking for in a brochure, how they're easiest to read, how they like to receive them. You will learn some valuable things.

- **Content**

  Whoever does the writing, the copy must be compelling, which won't guarantee that it will be read, of course, but those how do take the time to read it are more likely to become clients if what they read is professional and clear.

- **Format**

  Since most people don't usually take the time to closely read, your materials should be easy to skim. Use short paragraphs with simple, concise sentences. Bullets are perfect for products and services offered and for listing previous clients. Also, people want to know what they're reading before they read it. So give them headings to follow.

Promotional materials can come in a variety of shapes and sizes. Usually we think of a standard three-fold brochure. But because brochures that convey information concisely are most effective, I favor a two-fold for its simplicity, it gives you four sides to work with, which is usually plenty of space. And it offers the possibility of inserts, which can be useful if you need to highlight different parts of your business to different markets.

I also think that pocket brochures (basically a mini-folder) with inserted, graduated pages are valuable because again, they allow flexibility in the information you present. You include only those pieces which are appropriate for your prospect without burdening them with unnecessary and potentially overwhelming information.

Your materials should have:

- Details about the benefits of working with you or buying from your company
- A list of services and/or products offered
- Names of actual clients (if appropriate) or types of clients with whom you work
- Your company philosophy and what it's like to work with you
- Biographical information about the people behind the company
- Testimonials, always a very effective tool

A professional designer will give your materials a professional look and this is often crucial to the perception of your business. If you can't afford to hire a designer, at least find one to critique it for you before you print it. Also, it's ideal that designer and printer work together from the outset to create something coherent. Otherwise, you'll bring the designed piece to a printer who may quote you a price way out of line with what you anticipated and you'll have to go thru a design revision, which costs more time and money.

Alternative promo materials

- **Postcards**

  You can't get a lot of information on a postcard and sometimes that's the good news. I like postcards with bullets that just give the essential info. This is especially appropriate for service providers whose business is basically themselves.

- **Fact sheets**
  As the name implies, this piece – on a regular 8.5x11 page – just gives the facts: how long in business, services offered, list of clients as well as the answers to other questions your prospects routinely ask.

- **Intro letters**
  This should be (though rarely is) the easiest format because there's virtually no design involved. In a letter, you can include anything you'd put in a brochure but keep it to one page. The format is perfectly acceptable and professional.

Creating Materials That Don't Get Tossed

- **Don't rush**
  Creating excellent promotional materials, whether brochure, fact sheet or flyer, takes lots of time and requires meticulous detail work. That's one reason you need assistance. Once you've been working on it a while, you'll probably become tired of it and want it to be finished already. This is the very crucial point at which you need an outsider most.

- **Make materials worth keeping**
  In your materials, include information that is valuable to your prospect, not just stuff about you and your business. For example: A lawyer might include "Tips for First Time Home Buyers." A graphic designer could have "5 Design No-no's." A bookkeeper or accountant can keep prospects up to date on tax laws. Or a photographer can offer "How to take great vacation photos." The possibilities are endless.

- **Don't worry**
  Go ahead and give away some of your information. Clients don't hire you because they need your information (info is abundant!) They come because they can't (or don't want to) do it themselves. They need your help.

- **Sending it out**
  Don't send materials without a cover letter. And don't be afraid to repeat in your letter what's already in your brochure. In fact, repetition helps it to sink in.

Eight Brochure Don'ts

1. **Don't focus on facts instead of benefits.**
   For example, don't go into detail about the kind of equipment you use. Talk instead about the end-product they will see and buy.

2. **Don't use jargon.**
   big formal words or stilted language.

3. **Don't use dates.**
   They will soon make your brochure obsolete.

4. **Don't confuse your prospect with too much.**
   Simple, well-organized info is better.

5. **Don't forget to include yourself and the personality of your company in your brochure.**
   Otherwise, it will be dry and boring.

6. **Don't use an expository style exclusively.**
   Bullets are much easier to read.

7. **Don't send it to anyone cold, especially if it's expensive to produce.** Most people throw away the first thing you send them. Some feel they have to keep something that looks really expensive. Then they become resentful because they have to find a place to put it.

8. **Don't carry your brochure around or give it out at trade shows.** People often take too much info at events and then it ends up in a pile unread. Instead, hand out something small – your card or a postcard – get their card, and then follow up with your brochure.

CHAPTER 17 | TAKING THE COLD OUT OF COLD CALLING

Cold calling has a bad reputation, and so it should. I hate those pesky telemarketers who call me in the middle of dinner, have no idea whom they're calling, don't ask if it's a good time to talk and read from a script trying to convince me that I can't live without their new insurance policy or whatever.

Have you shied away from the phone for fear of coming off like a telemarketer? Or maybe, like me, you have phone fear.

I'd like to propose alternate ways to use the phone, other kinds of calls that can make it less painful, while keeping you in closer touch with your market and thereby increasing your business.

Develop a calling program that includes these three types of calls:
- **Research calls**
  gathering info, (sometimes known as prospecting)

- **Follow up calls**
  answering questions and reminding them of their interest

- **Maintenance calls**
  touching base and updating info

Research Calls Can Take the Sales Edge Off
Use the phone to gather info and to begin a relationship with your prospect or their screener-receptionist, secretary or assistant.

You don't have to speak to the actual person on the first call. In fact, it helps to make contact with the screener because they're the one who is likely to determine your fate. Get them on your side. They can be your advocate, your connection. Give them the power by asking for their help.

You're calling because you want to find out:

- If they have a need for your services
- Who you should speak to
- Are they happy with the person/company they're working with?
- If not, why not?

Try saying "I'm looking for some info. Perhaps you can help me." Wait for them to agree before you continue, "I'm wondering if you use (blank) services and, if so, I'd like to send some info about our company. Who would be the appropriate person?"

People are often willing to help you if they can and, if the timing is right, this type of call can turn naturally into a "sales call."

Follow up Calls Can Double Your Response Rate

I was recently invited to a cocktail party to preview the new collection of Maria Ficalora Knitwear. I got the invitation in the mail and considered going but was distracted by the next piece of mail, and soon forgot about it.

A week or so later, I got a follow up call from Maria's assistant asking if I was going to attend. Faced with a live person asking for a decision, I had to respond. I looked at my book and thought, "ok I'll go." If she hadn't called, the invitation would have languished in my in-basket for weeks. Because she called, I had to decide and the answer was "yes."

When to follow up

With the best intentions, people often end their letters with "I'll call you next week to follow up." But when the time comes, they don't call. This is very unprofessional.

Here's an alternative that doesn't commit you to anything you may not do: End your letter with, "Feel free to call with any questions. Otherwise I'll keep in touch." This leaves you open to follow up when and how you choose.

Let's say you meant to make follow up calls after a mailing but keep putting it off and now it feels too late. Not so fast...it's never too late. You can always call to follow up. Just say, "It's been a while since I send you that brochure so if you don't remember receiving it, I'll be happy to send you another."

If you're doing a big mailing and aren't making follow up calls because it would be overwhelming, try staggering the mailing (10/week or 50/week, whatever's manageable) so that the calls can fit into your day-to-day.

You want your name to be fresh in their mind when you call. Too soon and they may not have gotten to it yet – too late and they may have forgotten about it. I like to follow up a week after I send. Often, my info is sitting on their desk in a pile of unopened mail. The purpose of the call is to motivate them to look at it.

Maintenance Calls

The line between persistence and peskiness is a thin one. Your prospect has told you she is interested but not yet ready to get started. So you call every month and she's still not ready. Soon, you begin to feel like a pest because now she's not returning your calls.

How often is too often? Are three times enough – six times too many? I don't know but each of your prospects can tell you and often will, if you ask. If they say now isn't the time, ask when and how they'd like you to follow up.

I don't like people calling me regularly, so I always tell them to keep in touch via email or snail mail so I don't forget they exist. Other people don't mind saying no and prefer to get a regular phone call. Everyone's different.

Big Little Idea

Let a colleague make your calls and do the same for them. It's always easier to call about someone else's business, so find someone who has been putting off their research or follow up call and exchange lists. Do it together or separately.

Get their permission to send your email newsletter

If, like me, you hate to call someone without a reason, maintenance calls are for you. Try this: call everyone on your mailing list to get their email address and to ask permission to stay in touch by sending your monthly email newsletter. This will give you a reason to call and a complete email address book. If they seem willing to talk, ask them how their business is. The conversation could go anywhere!

Getting Over Phone Fear

I used to have phone fear. Here's one of my fears: I would call someone I haven't heard from in a while and I say, "Hi, this is Ilise Benun from Marketing Mentor" and they say nothing. Aaargh!

I also had a fear related to follow up calls but I got over it. Here's how:

Over the course of a year, I sent a few letters with ideas for articles to the editor of a trade magazine that I've written for in the past. She never responded so I assumed she wasn't interested. But as I worked on an issue of my newsletter, I decided to call her to follow up. And when I did, she said, "I'm so glad you called. I've been meaning to get back to you. I have your letter right here and I do like one of those ideas." I had an assignment before I got off the phone and there wasn't even an awkward moment of silence.

Be the Squeaky Wheel

People are increasingly bombarded with messages in all forms and from all sides. They've got piles on their desk and your material is probably in one of those piles. They've seen it, they want to contact you to find out more but other things take priority while your papers sit there fermenting on the desk.

Here's what could happen if you call to follow up: they pull the material out, focus on it then say, "Yes, let's get together," "I don't think this is right for me" or something in between. The idea is to keep the conversation moving.

People give attention to what's in front of them. So get in front of them.

Call First or Send First?

There is no right answer to this question but I've found that calling first is more effective.

Here's why:
- You plant the first seed. You have the opportunity to introduce yourself and find out if they are a prospect in the first place. This is recommended especially if your mailing piece is expensive.

- Calling gives you the chance to get the name and title of the right person. You may even be able to use the name of the person who directed you as a referral, which may lower their defenses slightly.

- You don't waste time, money and materials by sending to people who have no need for your product/services.

Nine Tips to Painless Phoning

1. **Tell them right away where you found them.**
   People become instantly more receptive when you begin by saying, "I got your name from..." Whether it's from a list, a colleague or the media, reveal your sources.

2. **Ask if it's a good time to talk.**
   Before you launch into your intro, be sure they're available. Your sensitivity and respect will be appreciated.

3. **Don't rush to speak with your prospect.**
   Get as much info from the screener as possible so that when you speak to the "buyer," they see you took the time to do your research.

4. **Get them talking and listen to the answers.**
   You don't have to do all the talking – in fact, you shouldn't. Ask the questions which uncover needs you can address directly, rather than wasting everyone's time on what you assume they need.

5. **Use a script or outline.**
   It helps to have a script but don't be locked into it. The purpose of a script is to guide you, to get you started, to provide structure. It can be especially helpful when your prospect doesn't respond as you expect, potentially causing you to forget your most important question.

6. **Set goals for how many people you'll call, not how many you'll get through to.**
   Don't get hooked on the number of responses. Just commit to making 5 or 10 calls a day. Or, if you prefer to get it all done at once, try 30 one morning a week (Tuesday, Wed and Thurs are good).

7. **Take notes during the conversation.**
   People feel heard if, in your follow up letter, you refer to something they said, especially personal details.

8. **Don't underestimate the value of leaving a message.**
   If it's a voicemail or answering machine message, you have the opportunity to make your pitch on the recording. If you leave a message with a live person, it gets your name in front of them one more time, even if they don't call you back.

9. **Reward yourself when it's over.**
   Chocolate, a special TV show, whatever does it for you.

Nine Tips for Voicemail Marketing

When they call you:

1. **Change your message often (I recommend weekly or daily).**
   This will encourage your prospects to actually listen to your message instead of zoning out. It will also make them feel that you are more accessible.

2. **Vary your tone of voice to make your message interesting.**
   This will also discourage them from letting their mind wander while they're waiting for the beep.

When you call them:

3. **Smile when you record your message.**
   They'll be able to hear it.

4. **Don't just leave your name and phone number.**
   Take a moment to explain why you're calling and let your prospect decide if they need what you're selling.

5. **Keep your message succinct.**
   Don't ramble on.

6. Speak slowly and spell everything.

7. Make sure you give them a compelling reason to return the call.

8. Let them know when it's convenient to call you back.

9. Don't make calls when you're in a bad mood.
    Your tone of voice may betray you and they may take it personally.

Voicemail Marketing

Whether you realize it or not, voicemail is a marketing tool that you can use at practically no expense.

When they call you

The goal of self promotion is to get the word out and this is best done when your prospect's defenses are down, which is generally the case when they're calling you.

Try this: for incoming calls, use your answering machine as a marketing tool by putting info about your company on your recording. Don't hesitate to include all or some of the following info bytes:

- A seven word blurb about the services and products you offer
- Your web site address
- Announcements about upcoming events
- Special discounts

Here are two sample messages that work for me:
"Hello, you've reached the Marketing Mentor and today is Thursday, Feb 10th. We're out of the office but we'll be sure to return your call as soon as we can. You can find out more right now if you go to www.marketing-mentor.com.

If you want to send a fax, the number is 201-222-2494. And for those of you who don't know, we offer a free, hour phone consultation which you can sign up for on the contact page of the web site. Leave us a message and thanks for calling."

If that's too long, try this:

Hello you've reached Marketing Mentor and today is Thursday, Feb 10th. We're out of the office but we'll be sure to return your call as soon as we can. You can visit our web site at www.marketing-mentor.com. And for those of you who missed it, we were recently featured in Crain's New Your Business. Just say so and we'll send you a copy. And thanks for calling.

When you call them

Now, look at voice mail from the other side. Let's say you're doing some marketing by phone – research or follow up calls – and your prospect isn't available. The receptionist asks, "Can I take a message or do you want their voice mail?"

When given the option, say "yes" to voice mail because it allows you to leave a detailed, private message. I especially prefer to record a message when I'm leaving info (simple or complex) because, like in the old game of telephone, it's always possible for details to get mangled in the transmission.

However, leaving messages on tape can feel futile. Many respondents to a survey said they prefer to leave a message on a tape rather than with a human being because it's more reliable. And while it may feel like voice mail jail when you're trying to reach a prospect, some respondents said they did get a call back when they do so. And I believe that if they're not returning your voice mail message, they wouldn't be returning the message you leave with a receptionist either. Although the latter is less frustrating, don't blame the tool for your prospect's unresponsiveness.

On the other hand, many otherwise conscientious people don't return calls these days simply because there are too many of them. Don't blame the people – blame the clutter!

Another Voice: Sue Yellin

If I'm an avid mailer, then Sue Yellin's my counterpart when it comes to the phone. When we first met, I though our approaches were polar opposite. Though our styles are different, I've recently come closer to sharing her views.

Here are some of Sue's tips:
- Exude confidence, credibility and enthusiasm

- Establish rapport

- Be succinct and interesting

- Be a great listener

- Uncover needs

- Ask for the appointment or the order

- Set goals for what you want to accomplish

- Make calls each week to develop momentum and continuity

- Design systems that make it easy to record data

- Follow up in a timely, organized manner

- Rejection is not personal

- Have fun -"they" are only people!

- There is business on the other end of the phone

CHAPTER 18 | NETWORKING IS TALKING ABOUT YOUR WORK

People often tease me because I'm always networking; but it's just that when someone asks what I do (and isn't that usually the first question?), I tell them…and guess what? That's networking – talking about my work, explaining to someone who's asked – what I do.

When it comes to talking about ourselves, many people are uncomfortable. It's almost as if it's not supposed to come from us. But people can't work with us if they don't know we're here. And if we don't tell them, who will?

In other words, networking is a timely exchange of selected bits of info about your business (not everything there is to all at once!) that you offer when someone is ready to hear it.

Being Visible

These days, there are tons of networking events to attend. Actually, there are too many events to attend, too many ways to meet yet another group of people you'll never see again.

The goal of networking is not to meet as many people as possible. The goal is to find a business community that satisfies your needs; one that brings together, first and foremost, the kind of people you're comfortable with and who are your prospects.

But joining a group isn't enough. Once you've chosen the community, you must be visible and participate in an ongoing way.

Networking Is...

Attending events is good; organizing events is even better, because that is how relationships develop – over time. Working with people on a project, so that the focus isn't on the relationship. Give people the chance to see you work and this kind of contact allows you to be there when their defenses are down. That's when it's possible to get to know someone. Other ways to participate include local politics, volunteer efforts for a charity, religious or spiritual groups, and hobbies or artistic activities. I even know someone who's made important contacts walking the dog.

I want to do more than exchange cards with a bunch of people. I go to these events with the intention of meeting someone I can chat with for a while, taking the time to learn about their business and tell them a bit about mine.

Sit down events, like breakfasts or lunches, are good, although there's always the fear of getting stuck next to someone who "can't do anything for you." However, the reality is that you can't tell by looking at someone what they do or who they know so I try to arrive with the attitude that Fate will seat me next to someone with whom, if we talk long enough, I will find something in common.

Recently I sat next to someone who seemed unfriendly at first; I was reluctant to even make a comment about the food. So I sat there in silence wishing I had picked a different table. Eventually, however, as more people sat down, we began talking. We exchanged cards, I followed up with a note, she called me to get together and now there are a few ideas about how we can work together. You just never know.

Finding Low-key Environments

Free events where the focus is on education are valuable not only because you have the opportunity to meet people but also because you can learn something. Be careful, though. It's too easy to be "the student" and then leave "class" as soon as it's over, without making contact with anyone. It only takes a little bit of courage, for example, to say "Wasn't that great?" to the person in the next row as you're getting up to leave.

Doing More Than Exchanging Cards

"Business card exchanges are too sharky!" So says Belinda Plutz, a consummate networker and owner of Career Mentors. I met Belinda at a NAFE (National Association of Female Executives) breakfast. Belinda asked the panelists a marketing question; so, assuming from her question that she would be open to hearing about self promotion, I approached her afterward and told her my thoughts about her question. And then I told her about my newsletter.

Thus the conversation began. She has since become a valuable resource. And, almost as a side effect, when someone comes to me asking for help with career change, you can be sure I will tell them about Belinda Plutz.

Don't Rush Away

Some of the best contacts I've made have happened after an event – in the bathroom, elevator or lobby of a building, or even on the street. That's when people's minds are open to it. That's when their defenses are down.

Tips for Business Wallflowers

"I just can't shove my card into someone's face"… If you've ever said that, here are some thoughts about how to make contact at networking events even if you're not "the assertive type".

- **Get there early.**
  If you get there when a lot of people are already there, you may think everyone is already talking to someone else. But if you arrive early, you'll have your pick of people to talk to.

- **Sit next to someone.**
  Don't sit alone, even if there are several empty chairs.

- **Ask questions of the speaker.**
  Or offer ideas and comments which reveal your business, your expertise, your experience. If people can refer or respond to something you said, that often gives them a reason and the comfort necessary to approach you (like I did with Belinda).

- **Look for other wallflowers.**
  Remember: most people are as uncomfortable as you are. They'll surely be grateful to have someone to talk to.

- **Stand by the food.**
  When people don't know what to do, they often eat. This is a good place to find people and the food offers a good "entrée" into conversation.

- **Wear something unusual.**
  This isn't for everyone, but sometimes it helps in the follow up process to distinguish yourself by saying "I was the one in the bright orange scarf." Or it could be a funny pin or an interesting tie or whatever is "you".

"I Don't Know What to Say..."

It doesn't really matter what you say. The goal is simply to make contact, even though it sometimes feels impossible. Here are some ideas of what to say to break the ice. Remember: anything can get a conversation started.

- **Introduce yourself.**
  Although it feels painfully awkward to some people, there's nothing wrong with "hi, my name is ___"

- **Ask a question.**
  Shift the focus away from yourself. People love to talk about themselves and they'll give you information you can use when it's time to describe your business.

- **Try these questions:**
  - What business are you in?
  - Who are your clients?
  - Why did you choose this event?
  - How was your day?

- **Talk about the food.**
  "What do you suppose that thing is?" (for mystery food).

- **Talk about the event.**
  - "This is my first time here."
  - "I really hate these things, don't you?"
  - "I'm still half-asleep." (most appropriate for early morning events)

- **Use the nametags.**
  If someone's nametag is undecipherable or unclear, ask what it means. Also, try putting something interesting and revealing on yours, which may encourage others to ask.

Keeping in Touch

Don't even bother collecting cards if you don't have a way to keep in touch. Whether it's as basic as a holiday card or a more consistent email marketing campaign or series of postcards, you must have a way to maintain contact.

CHAPTER 19 | ALL ABOUT LINKING

If you already have (or have begun) to create a Links Page, you understand the importance of having a web site that offers your visitors access to quality information. But the links on your Web site are only half the picture. The next goal of your linking strategy should be to pursue links from those key sites where your prospects are apt to be browsing. That way, you benefit from the exposure of these sites, which ultimately means more traffic to your own site. Getting those links is what this chapter is all about.

There Are All Kinds of Links

Basically any Web site or online medium that reaches your target market, and offers links, is potentially a place for you to get your site linked.

As for what kind of links you can hope to get, there are, of course, search engines and directories, where the results to any search provides links to resulting sites. But that's just the tip of the iceberg. For almost any industry, there are related directories and portals, trade publications and association sites, project/freelance database sites; regional directories – many of which offer listings and links to their members.

Complementary sites that have good linking potential for you include those sites that are within, or closely aligned to, your area of expertise, but whose focus is different. These could be the sites of colleagues, informal contacts, clients or strangers. Even so-called competitors will sometimes offer links.

Linking for Credit

If it's true that "content is king" on the Web (and it is), another means of getting links is to provide material, such as articles about any related topic, to the many sites hungry for informational content. A link to your site in the credit line is one of the ways you get compensated.

For more visually-oriented professions, there are online galleries and portfolios which accept graphic art content. And of course, links can always be added to email messages and blog postings.

Exactly how you go about getting strategic links is what we'll be looking at in this chapter, *"All About Linking"*. If your expectations for this kind of exposure are realistic – that a linking campaign is part of an overall effort to increase your online visibility and credibility, rather than to generate hot leads – you'll be pleasantly surprised by the connections you can make.

How to Find the Right Sites

When doing a strategic link development campaign, begin your research of potential sites with the most obvious element: sites that offer the same product or service as yours. Though competitive, they may also be complementary to yours.

Next, look for less obvious categories of sites to approach – quality content sites. For instance, a campaign for a site that sells antique jewelry would first target jewelry web sites – or antique collector-centered sites (including auction house sites), as well as estate sale sites.

The next level might include bridal sites, high-end department store or gift sites, and prop house/window display/costuming sites.

To find linking possibilities, use editor-driven directories and specialized search engines such as LookSmart.com, About.com and SearchEngineGuide.com and online publications for site ideas.

Concentrate on other sites with good links pages, and/or resource-heavy, industry portal sites.

For instance, our antique jewelry retailer might search the Jewelry and Retail Industry Guide (www.jewelers-choice.com/jewelryguide) and Sotheby's (www.sothebys.com) for potential linking sites.

This research takes time because it's often impossible to tell from a name and link description exactly what a Web site is like, or whether it even includes links. So be persistent and follow through.

Offer Something that Matters

The success of your linking campaign will depend on a variety of factors, but the most fundamental is that other site owners must be convinced that a link to your site adds value to theirs.

Here's where all your work on your own Links Page comes in, because no site is going to post a link to another site which essentially just says "buy my stuff." Plus, some sites can't or won't link to commercial sites (many nonprofits, for instance), so the more useful the content you offer, the more "non-commercial" you may appear to your potential linker.

Three Things Getting Links from Other Web Sites Does for Your Site

1. **Links increase traffic.**
   By exchanging or securing links with reputable industry sites, you create more opportunities to be seen online. Links also allow you to build bonds with sites that may have more exposure and stronger connections than you do to the markets you're after.

2. **Links boost your credibility.**
   Links from the Web sites of respected colleagues are the equivalent of online endorsements, which is essential in a place as anarchic, unstructured and vast as the Internet.

3. **Links allow you to participate in relevant communities.**
   Links are the heart and soul of the Web; by having your site well-linked, you're facilitating a community of complementary organizations who understand that "being connected" and making use of the Web's unique power is the best way for everyone to achieve their online promotional goals.

Top Ten Questions to Ask Yourself

In choosing link request targets, carefully evaluate their worth to you and your prospects by asking yourself these questions:

1. Is the website relevant to my product or service?

2. Do I want my site/business associated with this site?

3. Is it a quality site in terms of content and philosophy?

4. Is it well designed for its audience (i.e., easy to navigate, straightforward, well organized?)

5. Does it load quickly, or do the graphics make it too slow to be useful?

6. What sort of traffic does it seem to attract?

7. Do other sites link to/from it? If so, what kind of sites are they?

8. What can I expect to get out of a links from the site?

9. Is my site going to be worthwhile and appealing to visitors for this site?

10. Does my site offer another level of information of accessibility for the online community I'm helping to build?

How to Approach Sites for Links

Placing a link is a cinch; all you need is a simple line of HTML code. The hard part of a linking campaign is the personal aspect of getting a real person to place that link from their site to yours. It's not usually enough to say, "Link to my site." Even asking nicely doesn't always work. You must give them a reason to link, and the best reason to offer is that a link to your site would add value to theirs – which is why it's so necessary to have good content, such as a Links Page of your own.

Once you've identified and thoroughly looked through some sites to approach, create your generic (yet easily personalized) Link Request Message, which should include:

- The site and/or organization name

- A link to your Web site (so the webmaster can easily evaluate your site)

- The direct URL (Web address) of the page you want linked (your Links Page, or a page with an article, or your Homepage, etc.)

- A one or two line description of your site (make sure to have a 25-word version - directory sites require this)

- A sentence or short list of the benefits a link to your site offers to another site's visitors

Detailed Link Request Example

Dear WeWrite.org Webmaster:

I'd like to request that you consider adding a link to the Writers Studio site (http://www.writerstudio.com) on your Online Resources Page. This link would offer your visitors a unique and informative resource for improving craft in fiction and poetry writing.

Here are some of the features a Writers Studio link would offer your members and browsers:

- *A Poets & Writers article elaborating on the WS perspective on the importance of craft in powerful, "realized" writing*

- *A sample of the school's newsletter, in which students and faculty share with fellow writers their thoughts on the experience of writing*

- *A carefully selected collection of Web sites and resources invaluable to the creative writer, including literary/informational organizations, reference sites, art advocacy group sites, and online independent booksellers*

- *Information about the school's international Tutorials program, as well as ongoing class and two-day intensive workshop details*

Please contact me should you need any further information regarding either The Writers Studio or its Web site.

Thanks in advance,

Linking is About Relationships

Many sites are maintained by Webmasters working on a part-time basis who can't spend time figuring out where your link should go. This is especially true in the public sector/nonprofit world, as well as the consultant and small business world. Here are some tips to help you make it easy for them to link to you:

1. **Check for instructions.**
   Before you approach the Webmaster, check their links page listings for submission instructions to ensure that your description falls within the required parameters so your link request isn't overlooked. If you know HTML, you might also provide the code for your site's name/description. This allows the Webmaster to simply cut and paste to add the link.

2. **Suggest a category.**

   If the site you're approaching has its own categorized Links Page, tell the Webmaster where you think the link to your site belongs. Sometimes they will suggest another category, but the idea is to make the process as simple as possible for them, and to control your own "positioning" on the site.

3. **Include a description of your site that they can use.**

   This gives you more control over what your link will say. A link to "Angie's Antique Jewelry-Specializing in women's bracelets and watches from the '20s thru the '40s. Search our index by gem, metal, style or date" will tell them more than a bare bones link to "Angie's Antique Jewelry"

4. **Do a little each day**

   It's labor-intensive, so just do a little every day of the researching and compiling appropriate Web sites, then sending your personalized (yet generic) introductory message to the sites you've found. If you don't receive any response in a week, contact them a second time. You might also confirm you've got the right contact information by calling or visiting the site again.

5. **Keep track of your email requests**

   Also, double check the sites in a few weeks to see if a link to your site was added, even if you got no response.

Perseverance is important, but as with any potential relationship, move on if after a few weeks you seem to be getting nowhere.

A Link is an Endorsement

It's important to remember that it's quality more than quantity you're after when planning your linking campaign. Where you're linked reflects on you as much as those sites you've added to your own Links

Page. Being linked to a high-traffic site is only useful if the site is respected and popular, and gets the kind of traffic that's likely to bear you prospects. So if a link to your site appears on, say, a colleague's site whose work you both respect and think complements your own, then that link goes a long way toward endorsing you and your Web site.

Linking is Community-Building

Contacts, support, mentoring, information and services – that's part of what a true community should offer, on the Web or in the real world. Online, terms like "partners" and "affiliates" are thrown around a lot. But in the context of niche-driven, strategic linking, partnering refers to the process of forming relationships within the bigger picture of Web-based communities. Groups of businesses that can offer each other a network by linking, when it makes sense philosophically and strategically, are empowered to help each other achieve long-term goals.

Link Locally

- Is there a business-to-business online directory on the Web site for your town or city?

- Can you exchange links with other local businesses whose expertise complements your own? For an online listing of US chambers of commerce, go to www.Chamber-of-commerce.com

- Does your trade association or professional organization offer links to members' Web sites? For national directories of associations, check out: www.Associationcentral.com

Linking is a Way to Combat the Inevitable Fees for Search Engine Placement

According to Eric Ward, writing in B2B Magazine, "Like it or not, if you want your site listed and linked at the major search engines and directories, you will, sooner or later, have to pay for that privilege." And while it hurts having to pay for what was once free, it's a wonder it was ever free to begin with.

Just remember that aside from search engines and directories, every day, millions of people find Web sites without ever going near a search engine. They find them through plain old links on smaller vertical Web guides, link lists and industry directories. So get busy and build a network of links. That's still free.

Do's And Don'ts of Linking

The Four Things Every Links Page Should Have
Remember, your links page is part of the overall content of your site, not a throwaway page, so treat the material within as you would the rest of your site.

1. **Categories.**
   If you plan on having more than just a few links (and there's no point in having a links page if you don't), some kind of structure is key to keeping visitors from being overwhelmed and clicking off. Arrange your links by industry or some other category, and put them in some kind of order.

2. **URL or Web address.**
   When this is "hidden" within the HTML code of the site, people can click on it but can't type it in, like this: The Art of Self Promotion

   Sometimes, the complete web address may be given, like this: http://www.artof selfpromotion.com

   If you're trying to decide whether to show the whole URL, don't worry that you're giving away precious information that jeopardizes your own chance of getting clients. Making it easy to link will ultimately add to your site's value, thereby increasing your chances of return or word-of-Web-inspired visits (especially if you update your links page periodically).

3. **Name of the organization and/or Website.**
   People like to know where they're going, so tell them the company name, especially if it's not obvious from the Web address.

4. **A one-line descriptor.**
   Write one or two lines describing the link you're offering. Focus on what you like about the site and what it does well; offering your point of view enables you to become a guide for your visitors. This also increases your site's value and helps to position you as an expert.

The Ideal Link

So the ideal link looks something like this:

http://www.gladwell .com
This is the Web site of Malcolm Gladwell, author of the best seller, The Tipping Point. This book is about how to spread word of mouth on a budget, and includes many fascinating concepts about how hot trends and social epidemics spread through a society. Highly recommended! Read excerpts from the book here: http://www.gladwell.com/

Yes, it's true that every link you add to your site is a doorway to another location, an escape hatch that moves the visitor out of your information space and into another. And once visitors make that escape, they may not return to your site at all. So while you want to enhance your credibility and value by helping your visitors find related resources, you don't want to show them the exit to your site before you have a chance to show your own stuff. Try these linking techniques:

- **Don't put links on your home page.**
  Give visitors a chance to see what you're offering first. Put your links on pages that are nested at least one level below the home page of your Web site, so visitors will be exposed to some of your own information before they can head for the door.

- **Check out each resource yourself before linking to it.**
  It's easy to grab a cool-sounding URL out of a magazine, from an email message or discussion group post, but you should always check out the resource yourself before including it. The URL may be wrong, or gone, or the site may contain material that's detrimental to your own marketing efforts.

- **Link to sites that augment, rather than compete with, the information you're offering.**
  Look for sites that offer more detail about a subject your site touches on. For example, at one point the Web site of Melissa Galt's Atlanta-based interior design firm, Linea Interiors (www.lineainteriors.com) offered a very comprehensive page of links that went into more depth about home furnishings than she did on her Web site. Her Resources Page extended into categories such as Home Furnishing and Accessories Resources, Expertise on Home Improvement, Bed and Linens Sources and Appraisers. The short, one-line descriptor of each link was also very helpful.

  This text was adapted from the Weekly Guerilla article by Charles Rubin

CHAPTER 20 | EMAIL

How to Get Your Email Messages Read

Email comes so fast and furiously that it's all I can do to surf mine. Who has time to actually read it? So anticipate that your email messages will not get the close reading they would on paper, and write them with that in mind. The following essential elements for your email messages will help.

The Five Essential Elements of Your Email Messages:

The fate of your email messages – read, deleted or left to languish – is determined by the following five elements:

1. **The "To" Field:**
   You know how people look at the address label on their snail mail to see who the mail they get is actually addressed to? They're doing the same with email. They're looking at the "to" field to find out who else is getting the email messages they are receiving. And if it's not addressed directly to them (and only them), they are less likely to read it. So if your message is being sent to more than one person, you should either use the blind carbon copy for your recipients, or, if it's a small list, send one message at a time. You will get better results.

2. **The "From" Field.**
   This is what I look at first and use to decide whether or not to delete an incoming email message. If it's not from someone I know, or at least from a name I recognize, I may not even look at the subject line. So make sure your name (not your email address) comes up in the "from" field of your email messages.

3. **The Subject Line.**

    Use your subject line to answer questions like "What is this message about? What does your recipient have to do and when? What kind of response is required?" These details should, of course, also be included in your message, but distill them into your subject line, just in case that's all your recipient sees.

4. **The Text Above the Fold.**

    Many email programs allow the recipient to see the beginning of an incoming message without actually opening it. So be sure that the essence of your message is conveyed in the first few lines. Don't bury it near the end.

5. **Your Signature (or Sig) File.**

    When your prospects are in their moment of need, not only must they think of you, they must also be able to contact you without wasting too much time. Your sig file, the electronic equivalent of your letterhead, can achieve this. Most email programs allow you to attach text (and sometimes an image file) to the end of every message you send. Make sure yours includes all your contact info (who you are, what you do, where you are located, and how you can be reached). This will make it supremely easy for prospects to get in touch.

Send Only One Thought per Message

Because people often judge the relevance of an email message by what they see "above the fold," if you address another issue further down in the message, or add a PS at the bottom, it's likely they won't ever see it.

So keep your message focused. Offer one idea, comment or question per message – two at the most. If you have more to say on other topics, sent multiple messages with clear subject lines. That way, your recipient can deal with each issue separately and then file the messages in appropriate folders.

How to Turn Email into "Me-mail"

Recently, I needed to find a photographer fast. I didn't have time to do a search anywhere, not online, not in my piles of papers or my filing cabinet, or even in my database. I had no time to establish trust; I needed to already know that the person I chose would be capable.

The first place I looked was in my email inbox. You know why? It required the least time and effort because it was right there in front of me.

And in my inbox I found – eureka! – an old email message from a photographer thanking me for a workshop I'd given. His message had his name, his email address, and his phone number (and I'd already seen examples of his work) – so I had everything I needed to schedule the appointment, which I did, then crossed that off my list.

I don't think I'm the only one using my inbox this way. So if your clients are too, there had better be a message from you handy when they are in their moment of need.

Me-mail, not Spam

I'm a strong proponent of email marketing because it works for me and I've seen it work for others. But it must be done responsibly, respectfully and thoughtfully. Seth Godin, author of *Permission Marketing,* coined the term "me-mail", which he defines as *"email that is anticipated, personal and relevant."* That's the kind of email people don't mind getting. In this chapter, we will look at the different ways small business owners are using me-mail to stay connected and keep in touch with their markets.

But first, just a few words about spam:

Spam is Relative

While email marketing is a hot topic, there are some very vehement opinions out there against it.

Look, we all get more email than we want, and if we had more time to spend reading what comes in, much of it would probably not be considered spam, because there is a lot of useful information floating out there in cyberspace.

And although I do get a lot of junk, there are some email messages that I really appreciate because they offer me a perspective or access to resources that I can't get anywhere else.

That's what you must offer your recipients, and if you do, they may actually thank you, instead of cursing you.

Email Marketing Strategy #1
Send Regular Updates About Your Business

Believe it or not, your prospects and clients do want to hear from you. If you don't believe me, listen to what Leisa Kennedy, of Belo International, a Texas-based media corporation, has to say: *"My friends at Sibley Peteet Design send me new work via email and I like that. I want to see what they come up with next. I'm surprised more designers don't send email."*

Your clients are interested because they are likely to be in need of your products and services at some point, and they want you to keep in touch with them. So the easiest email marketing campaign you can mount is one in which you periodically show examples of your latest projects.

Every other month, Newport Beach, Ca-based Lecoursdesign designs promotional email messages (with image files attached) as a way of showing what they're working on. Here's a recent example:

News from Lecoursdesign
Our firm was recently tasked with the design of an identity for a new venture named ZEROg Products. We developed the attached wordmark to communicate the progressive, scientific, and healthy nature of ZEROg. This was accomplished through custom typography and a superscript "g" connoting scientific notation.

The g floats in zero gravity, hence ZEROg. Ice-blue and metallic sliver give it a technical, yet light feeling.

ZEROg Products produces "problem solving products," a tagline developed by Lecoursdesign. Their first creation is an ergonomic backpack that evenly distributes the load to reduce fatigue.

Lecoursdesign specializes in not-necessarily corporate identity, brand identity, print collateral, and web design. Call us and see how we can creatively enhance the perception of your organization.

Not only did the message prompt prospects to respond, but one person offered some valuable feedback as well as an invitation to meet.

How to Send Regular Updates

1. Compile a list of clients and prospects with whom you already have a relationship (i.e. people who know your work).
2. Decide what to send them. Here are some ideas for messages:
   - Quick tips about anything related to your field of expertise
   - Links to useful (or merely interesting) resources you've come across
   - Details on what's new with you and your business

You can even use email to advise prospects and clients about your travel schedule, or to let them know when you are available to take on new projects.

Anyone who sends out regular mailings, whether promotional postcards, newsletters, or calendars, swears by the results they achieve by keeping in touch with their target market.

That's the idea behind email marketing. It's basically direct mail on the Internet, but even more effective because it requires so little effort for clients to respond. It keeps you top-of-mind, keeps your market connected to you, and most important, the succession of communication solidifies relationships between you and your prospects.

Email Marketing Strategy #2

Send Monthly tips to Self-subscribed Prospects

Another way to use email marketing is to send regular messages that serve two purposes: to educate your prospects and clients about your field, and to position you as an expert in it.

That's one of the goals behind The Levison Letter, a monthly email newsletter of Action Ideas for Better Direct Mail, Email, Web Sites & Advertising sent out by direct response copywriter, Ivan Levison.

The Levison Letter started on paper in 1987, but in 1999 Levison made the switch to digital distribution and now has several thousand self-subscribed readers from more than 37 countries within the high-tech industry. He writes his monthly messages in a very personable tone and covers marketing topics like, "How to Write for the Web."

And Levison isn't shy about using his email newsletter as a marketing tool. Each issue begins with a request to forward the message to colleagues (which generates additional exposure), and ends with a pitch for his services and a call to action. Here's an excerpt from a past message:

Write it right in the Year 2000 – Five resolutions for high-tech marketers

1. *Keep it simple. Your prospects don't want to think about your message. They want to understand, QUICKLY, exactly what your product or service can do for them. So don't use long sentences when short ones will do. Don't use long words when short ones will do. Explain benefits clearly. Strip off the verbal fat and write rock-hard, muscular prose that gets results.*

2. *Keep it short. Some years ago, I used to write long selling-letters for clients. "The more you tell, the more you sell" was my watchword. And the long stuff pulled just great. Now, things are changing. Readers are less patient. Their attention spans are shorter. Which means that the sales letters, email, etc. I write are getting shorter*

too. Does this move to a shorter format bother me? Absolutely not! The only thing any direct response writer should care about is what WORKS.

Ilise, want me to create some "salesmanship in print" for YOU? Give me a call and let's talk. Or send me an email. I write for Adobe, Apple, Claris, Hewlett-Packard, Intuit, Intel, Microsoft, Netscape and many other terrific companies. Why not you? If you need me to write sales letters, email letters, ads, Web content, whatever, please get in touch anytime. And if you haven't done so already, check out http://www.levison.com.
All will be revealed!

Email Marketing Strategy #3
Send Email Press Releases to Press Contacts, Clients and Colleagues
Jeff Fisher. of LogoMotives, a Portland, Oregon-based corporate identity firm, considers himself a shameless self promoter. He estimates that three quarters of his business comes through word-of-mouth. But Fisher isn't sitting around waiting for the phone to ring. He keeps in touch.

In the old days, he used snail mail; now he does it online – with his Web site, email messages and email press releases. Twice a month, Fisher sends out an email press release announcing awards he has won, new clients he has taken on, or projects he has completed.

These email press releases, with the whimsical subject line of TOOT TOOT, are sent to editors and writers of local business journals, such as *Oregon Business and Media Ink,* a Seattle trade publication for creative industries.

Cesar Diaz, a writer at the Oregonian who has used several of Fisher's releases in their Business section, likes getting press releases via email. *"That way I can look at it on my own time and decide what to do with it,"* he says.

And here's the proof that email PR works. One result of these twice-monthly mailings is that two major Oregon papers did feature stories on Fisher's work in 1999. *"The story in The Oregonian resulted in 20 new clients immediately, and seven months later I am still getting calls,"* boasts Fisher.

Incredible results, indeed, but that's not all. Print publicity can also translate directly into online publicity, completing the circle. A mention of LogoMotives in the Business section of The Oregonian was also included in the paper's online edition and is archived indefinitely on the publication's Web site.

Fisher doesn't stop there. Getting the most out of his marketing effort, he also sends his press releases to his email marketing list, which is made up of his clients and vendors, networking pals (other designers) and friends, *"because you just never know."*

Here is an excerpt form one of Fisher's email press releases:

Work by Jeff Fisher Logomotives featured on Eyewire.com Gallery

Two logo designs by Jeff Fisher LogoMotives have been added to the online gallery of EyeWire.com

Eyewire is one of the leading Internet and mail-order sources for stock photography, illustration, video footage, audio clips, fonts and software for the graphic design industry. Their online gallery features work by a variety of designers using products from the Eyewire catalog. The gallery can be found at www.eyewire.com/magazine/gallery/you/ (click on the graphic of the plate).

The examples designed by Jeff Fisher include the logo design for Glo's Broiler, a restaurant in Seattle. The symbol uses the Eyewire font Frankfurter in conjunction with graphic elements representing a plate of food and a checkered tablecloth. The logo has also been featured in the

Japanese graphics book "New Logo and Trademark Design" and the recent publication "Bullet-proof Logos."

Fisher has designed over 50 logos for the Portland theater company in the past ten years – winning 20 design honors in the process.

Jeff Fisher
Engineer of Creative Identity
Jeff Fisher LogoMotives
PO Box 17155
Portland, OR 97217-0155
Phone: 503-283-8673 Fax: 503-283-8995
Email: jeff@jfisherlogomotives.com
Website: www.jfisherlogomotives.com

*If I don't "toot!" my own horn no one else will.

Email Marketing Strategy #4
Use Email to Start a Conversation

Cold email marketing is simple: you send an introductory email message to a prospect out of the blue. Horrifying, right? Not if you target carefully, write concisely and approach people respectfully.

This is not about mass emailing. It's about finding a way to approach, one at a time, the prospects you really want to work with and whom you know need your services and products.

This technique will help you initiate a conversation that just may turn into something beautiful, but only if you reach out.

Each time writer and photojournalist Jed Block does email marketing he gets at least one job – and a job that he would not have gotten otherwise. In fact, that's what happened when he sent a message to Mary Kramer of K&G Tax Consultants.

Here's the message he sent:

Hey Mary:

I just updated my Web site and thought you'd be interested in an exercise that appears under "Current Piece of Work." If you haven't visited for awhile, I invite you to look around the site, It's not all business – most of the time, I try to have a little fun.

This is a one-time mailing that I thought might interest you. If you'd like to stay in touch, the site makes it easy for you. And please don't hesitate to contact me if I could ever help out.

Thanks,
Jed Block,
Who writes for business and people wanting to communicate clear, stimulating, professional information to others. http://www.jedblock.com

Kramer was very receptive to Block's message and has since hired Block to work on several projects, including the firm's Web site.

"What grabbed me," she says, *"was that all his message did was introduce his Web site. It wasn't a big pressure thing. Plus, we had been thinking about doing a Web site for a year, and we were looking for help. So when I got the message, I looked at his site."*

And the rest, as they say, is history.

How to Do Cold Email Marketing That Gets a Response

1. Choose your prospect carefully and find their email address. Make sure it's someone who fits into your target market.

2. Send a brief message – no more than three sentences, which includes this information:

    a. Who you are and what you offer (your tagline or 7-word blurb is prefect for this).

    b. How they can find out more about your services or products.

    c. The question you want them to answer (probably related to whether they use services like yours).

If you have done your homework and if you are truly offering something your recipient can use, then all it takes is one click for your prospect to say, "Yes, tell me more."

And if they don't respond, you've lost nothing but a few moments of time.

About Ilise Benun

Ilise Benun is an author, consultant, speaker and founder of Marketing Mentor. She is the author of 3 books: "Stop Pushing Me Around: A Workplace Guide for the Timid, Shy and Less Assertive" (Career Press 2006), "Self-Promotion Online" and "Designing Web Sites:// for Every Audience" (HOW Design Books), and co-author of "Public Relations for Dummies, 2nd Edition" (Wiley, 2006).

Her work has been featured in national publications such as *Inc. Magazine, Nation's Business, Self, Essence, Crains New York Business, Dynamic Graphics, IQ (a Cisco Systems magazine)* and *Working Woman, The New York Times, Toronto Globe and Mail, The Denver Post* and more.

Benun publishes a bi-weekly email newsletter called "Quick Tips from Marketing Mentor," which is read by 8000+ small business owners and has been excerpted in many other email newsletters, including Bob Bly's *Direct Response* Letter and Michael Masterson's *Early to Rise*.

Benun's articles about marketing (with links to her 3 web sites) are posted on sites all over the Internet, including: Early to Rise, Slate.com, ClickZ.com, Jim Blasingame's SmallBusinessAdvocate.com, StrategicBusinessNetwork.com, Smallbiztechtalk.com, Marketingsherpa.com, RecognizedExpert.com, Marcommwise.com, BusinessBooksandMore.com, Freelancewriting.com, Creativebusiness.com, Creativelatitude.com, as well as sites for trade organizations such as Usability Professionals' Association (upassoc.org), Design Management Institute (dmi.org), Advertising Photographers of America (apanational.org), American Design Awards, Howdesign.com and many more.

Benun has conducted workshops and given presentations for national and international trade organizations, including American Marketing Association (several local chapters), International Association of Business Leaders, American Consultants League, Business Marketing Association, the National Association of Women Business Owners (several local chapters), the Family Business Council, American Writers and Artists Institute, AIGA (several local chapters), Graphic Artists Guild (several local chapters), NJ Creatives, Registered Graphic Designers of Ontario, NY Designs - a program of LaGuardia Community College/CUNY, the NYU Entrepreneurship Summit, Editorial Freelancers Association, WorldWIT (Women in Technology), the Usability Professionals Association (several local chapters), the HOW Design Conference, NY Public Library, the 92nd St. Y and many ad clubs around the country.

Through her Marketing Mentor program, founded in 2004, Benun works closely with the creatively self employed to teach them the "marketing mindset," which includes how to get out of your own way, how to make connections with prospects, how to fit self-promotion into your day-to-day life and how to avoid Feast or Famine.

Benun is also a board member of the Usability Professionals' Association (NY Chapter) and Women in Cable and Telecommunications (NY Chapter).

She started her Hoboken, NJ-based consulting firm in 1988 and has been self-employed for all but 3 years of her working life. She has a B.A. in Spanish from Tufts University.

More info here: http://www.marketing-mentor.com